AS LONG AS I KNOW YOU

as long as

THE MOM BOOK

The Sue William Silverman Prize for Creative Nonfiction

I Know You

ANNE-MARIE OOMEN

THE UNIVERSITY OF GEORGIA PRESS & ATHENS

Published by the University of Georgia Press
Athens, Georgia 30602
www.ugapress.org
© 2022 by Anne-Marie Oomen
All rights reserved
Designed by Kaelin Chappell Broaddus
Set in 10/13.5 Dolly Pro Regular by Kaelin Chappell Broaddus
Printed and bound by Versa Press
The paper in this book meets the guidelines for permanence
and durability of the Committee on Production Guidelines for
Book Longevity of the Council on Library Resources.

Most University of Georgia Press titles are
available from popular e-book vendors.

Printed in the United States of America
26 25 24 23 22 P 5 4 3 2 1

Library of Congress Cataloging-in-Publication Data

Names: Oomen, Anne-Marie, author.
Title: As long as I know you : the mom book / Anne-Marie Oomen.
Description: Athens : The University of Georgia Press, [2022]
Identifiers: LCCN 2022002704 | ISBN 9780820362540 (paperback ; alk. paper) | ISBN
    9780820362557 (ebook)
Subjects: LCSH: Oomen, Anne-Marie. | Adult children of aging parents—United States—
    Biography. | Mothers and daughters—United States—Biography. | Parent and adult
    child—United States. | Aging parents—Care—United States. | Dementia—Patients—
    Family relationships.
Classification: LCC HQ1063.6 .O66 2022 | DDC 306.874/092—dc23/eng/20220127
LC record available at https://lccn.loc.gov/2022002704

TO MY MOTHER, Ruth Jean Oomen,
APRIL 28, 1921–NOVEMBER 16, 2020
AND TO ALL THOSE IN THE "HOMES"

Dark on a bright day, fear of you is two-poled,
Longing its opposite. Who were we?
What for? dreaming, I haunt you unconsoled.

—MARIE PONSOT, "Late"

CONTENTS

ACKNOWLEDGMENTS

- To Laure-Anne Bosselaar for the Brown-Bosselaar Le Petite Studio residency in April 2019, where I finished the first full draft of the manuscript.
- To Katey Schultz for inviting me to the Interlochen Writers Retreat at the Interlochen College of Creative Arts, where I served as Writer in Residence from 2017 to 2020 and where I worked on the manuscript in various stages. And again to Katey for her invitation to Arrowmont School of Arts and Crafts winter residency, Pentaculum 2018, where for the first time the unruly pieces shaped themselves into an order. Thanks also to the writers and artists whose company there inspired me, especially Suzi Banks Baum.
- To members of my writers' groups who saw many early drafts of individual chapters: Karen Anderson, Gail Bozzano, Fleda Brown, Bronwyn Jones, Mardi Link, Patricia Ann McNair, Stephanie Mills, Cari Noga, Nancy Parshall, Julia Poole, Teresa Scollon, Heather Shumaker, Jen Sperry Steinnorth, and Catherine Turnbull. And to Karen Anderson again, for identifying the title of the book.
- To literary friends who through their work in both nonfiction and other genres affirmed or inspired the work along the way: Linda Nemec Foster, Niki Conraths, Ruth Nathan, Michael Steinberg, Keith Taylor, Lee Hope, Richard Hoffman, Dana McConnell, Jeanette Mason, and many others.

❧ To Meg Kearney for the Solstice MFA extended-stay residency, and to Solstice colleagues who have discussed this manuscript with me and helped me in various writerly ways: Tanya Whiton, Laure-Anne Bosselaar, Amy Hoffman, Steve Huff, Laura Williams McCaffrey, Renee Watson, Randall Horton, Kathi Aguero, Kassie Rubico, Quintin Collins, and Beth Little. And to Solstice students and alums who have asked about and listened as I searched for meaning.

❧ To Caitlin and Theo Early and to the sauna family and Beach Bards—Norm and Mimi Wheeler, Bronwyn Jones, Joe Vandermuelen, and sweaty friends in the spirit of story.

❧ To the doctors, nurses, volunteers, and aides who every day took care of my mother, both at Cherry Blossom Manor and at the remarkable Oceana County Medical Care Facility. They do the hardest, most challenging job in the world. They are generally not well paid for their skills. They should be. As the boomer generation ages toward our elder years, we will need more and more of these skilled caregivers. We need to respect the work they do, train them to the highest level, and provide them with good pay and benefits. We should have been doing this all along.

❧ To Great Lakes Hospice Care (now Elara Caring) and especially Nicki Alvesteffer for patience, kindness, and ongoing attention during the time they were involved in palliative care—before the pandemic cut their visits. They sang, prayed, attended, and monitored. Because of them, my mother had a better quality of life. Hospice presence also allowed me to continue to travel and to finish this book, which I hope helps readers better understand this journey, how we move toward the mysteries.

❧ To the Oomen family for their understanding that "re-remembering" memory is what I do, and especially to my sisters, Marijo Oomen Bakker and Pat Harpe, who lived much of this with me, but whose perspectives and memories will undoubtedly prove different. I am so grateful to them both for their love and for our mutual respect in the time of Momcare.

❧ To my beloved David Early: without you, pen doesn't touch paper. Always, always, with so much love.

Acknowledgment and sincere gratitude for publishing earlier versions of:

"My Mother's Country," *Solstice: A Magazine of Diverse Voices*, winter 2017 (with thanks to Lee Hope and Richard Hoffman).
"Buttons," Hypertext Literary Magazine, fall 2021 (with thanks to Christie Maul Rice).

NOTE TO READERS

Except for mine, my siblings', and my mother's name, most names have been altered. That said, compared to my other memoirs, the events described here are less blurred by the vagaries of memory and less free of educated guesses and most-likely details. I kept notes on many of these interactions as they happened, and I wrote early drafts of many chapters shortly after the incidents occurred. Still, for the sake of story, some incidents are differently ordered and dialogue is compressed, though the tone is replicated as closely as I remember. Finally, the interior meaning assigned to these incidents is mine alone. Suppositions about my mother's thoughts are based on a combination of my long history with her and on my habitual "listening" to her internal voice, which may or may not have been accurate—such are the uncertainties of meaning and memory. My mother was a powerful, mysterious, and utterly vulnerable human being who can no longer speak her anger or her forgiveness. Her generosity was often overshadowed. Except . . . our amorphous friendship, made possible only by her dementia, was a late-blooming sweetness I will cherish. Finally, my siblings' experiences of this time in our lives, in particular those of my sisters, Pat and Marijo, are inevitably different from mine, and rather than this being problematic, I suspect it enriches our understanding of our very complicated mother.

PROLOGUE: CESSATION

The breath. Or rather, the unbreath.

The calls to the family, done. The rush of reaching all five siblings, the questions to the doctors, the questions without answers, all done. In the CCU in Ludington Memorial Hospital, on the western knuckle of Michigan's high-five hand, my ninety-one-year-old father, my beloved and gentle father, is wrapped in the apparatus of crisis. We, the family—his wife, five adult children, numerous grandchildren—have gathered, standing around the bed that is strangled in tubes, standing in sudden understanding. At the head of the bed, my mother holds my father's hand. She and my sister Marijo embrace, and then Marijo, who is the one who can say these things, speaks directly to Dad, who is in some state here but not here: coma, drug-induced sleep, altered but still alive. She tells him that we love him, and then she says, "Dad, we are all here." Then she and Mom are holding each other again. I am watching them, relieved they have found the courage for this embrace after the tensions of the day, grateful for my sister's words. I am watching the monitors, the up/down gesture of the heartline.

That first cessation.

Am I at the foot of the bed, touching his feet as I have so often during this long day? Or am I at his side, with my hand touching lightly the edemic hands? I think I am studying my brothers' sturdy faces. Or perhaps I am watching Mom and Marijo. The room is crowded but oddly still, and in that sudden silence, my face turns toward his face as though someone cupped it and pulled it gently so that I would deliberately be shown the great round head, the wide brow, the nearly balding scalp, the face of the man who I think has been the most powerful person in my life, this fine father whom I have loved deeply. Who loved me deeply.

Then, breathing again. But now we attend, our attention tight and high, his breathing low and guttural. Something even older than breath is entering the room. We know. Some unshape in the suspension between breaths, the longer space filling between each. A parallel suspension among us. The monitors have gone to black.

The second cessation.

Inside that silence. Quiet like cotton. Quiet like fog. Quiet like done.

Then, as if someone struck a terrible blow to the room.

A deafening without a sound for being deafened.

Rush and spin in that breathlessness.

Then, not terrible. Only our loss is terrible, but the death is not terrible, simply unspeakable, something beyond anything we knew before this moment. Common, yes, but beyond beyond, beyond whatever it means to comprehend; not to be comprehended.

Death itself is quiet, its priestly work completed.

We stand in its presence for a while, dumb and numb, our hearts still beating.

Nurses enter the room on their quiet shoes. How did they know? Can they turn the monitors off in the room but keep them on at the station? Of course. They take pulse at feet, throat, wrist, thigh. Then the charge nurse, a woman in blue, her voice soft, calls into the dark hall, to someone with a clipboard, "Twenty-two thirty." I automatically calculate. Ten thirty at night.

She pauses at the door, takes us in. She says softly, "Take all the time you want."

Someone starts the Lord's Prayer. "Our father, who art in heaven." My mother adds the final phrase for the dead, "And let perpetual light shine upon him." We touch him. We tell him we love him. We kiss his forehead. My mother bends over him and sobs into his chest.

When is it that my mother stands up, hanging on to the bed railing, wobbly on her frail legs, and turns to say something to all of us. She gathers her breath. "His greatest wish was to have all of you return to the church." Does she look at me? I think she looks at me. Because my brothers have returned to the Catholic Church and brought with them their wives, and my youngest sister is in Africa right now with a mission group. And Marijo, while not a practicing Catholic, is more spiritual than the rest of us—and Mom knows this. So that leaves . . . me.

I stare, stunned. This is what she wants to say at a time like this? And to say it in such a way, as manipulation rather than last wish, to say that one thing that would mean I had disappointed my father. Everything I have tried to be to her and failed to be comes rushing back in wild heat. Everything of the past, the hard core of our troubles shimmers in the air with whatever is left of my father in that ceremony of dying. My thumb goes to my lips, chewing the nail, my breath hot with old anger rising again in biting my thumb. The claw is prevented from doing harm by tearing it away, piercing instead my own lip.

I don't say a word. Bite down.

Then, *Not on your life, not even for you, Dad.*

And then the skepticism: Did he really ask that? Would he have asked that? Or was that a long ago wish? Or did she make it up? So I would be who she wanted me to be? Again.

The world shifts back.

We are half orphaned. Our family stands in a hospital room that is a field of silence all about her. She remains now: mother, parent, elder, and now, widow. She is drive, control, shame, power, mourning, distorted love, love, love, all of it. And also, suddenly—I know this more deeply than anything—she is alone. And now, an intuition springs from connection that has always been knife sharp between us. Her solitude will be specific, demanding. And mothers should have that, these women who gave us life, who raised us up, who wiped our butts. But hers, hers is beyond me. For one simple reason: I have not been a good daughter. And I don't intend to start now. The pattern was set long ago and can't be marred by breath or unbreath.

Except I know nothing of the work of grief. Except I know nothing, really, of her.

BUTTONS

Childhood, rivered with need, with talk that pools under the talk that talks. Childhood is about money; not enough, not enough. Childhood is my dad wanting to plant some new field but there is no money for seed, the cows have been sick and the vet will not come, machinery is broken. Somewhere beyond us something called communism is spreading, and an atomic bomb might, right now, be in the air, falling. The Russians can do that. And there is no money. All this is in my mother and father's talk even when it is not. And now it seems we have a farmhouse of holes. My mother is worried about the holes, our shoes with holes, shirts with holes, sweaters and coats with tears like mouths open and panting. Holes. The fronts of our coats flap like doors in wind. Winter is coming.

I am not yet ten, but I have already been taught the world is round. In science class, I have seen the picture, pieced together parts of the world from those rockets that entered space for the first time and sent back the photos so if you strung them together, you could see the curve, supposedly proving at last that this place is not flat, but round. I don't believe it—too scary. I know it is false, like the fake money in Monopoly—it just looks a little real. The world is certainly no egg of iron and lava, as my science teacher has announced. If you climb the hill behind the barn, you see all the way to the lake, the edge. Flat.

"But then why does the lake disappear?" My mother argues with me. Her question is full of the holes where knowing lives.

Because you've come to the end of it, I think to myself.

Don't say it. Because where the sky starts, that's the end of the world. *Don't say it.* She'll be mad for my sassing.

As though she has read my mind, she says, "No. Something's always past the edge." And what happens there? My hands turn cold. The things I don't know. My heartbeat turns into the sound of rain. These are thoughts I get lost in when I am trying not to get lost in the worry about the holes.

In autumn, the time of loss, a farm auction near Hart, a farm that has "gone under." I don't know what that means but when it happens, everyone feels bad, but then everyone still goes to the auction, hoping stuff will be cheap enough to afford. My father is looking for a better plow. After rummaging around the household items for a long time, my mother buys a round box, gray with time, a faded red rim and a gray ribbon stretched across the dust-shadowed top. No one else wanted it so it's cheap. She calls it a hatbox but it doesn't hold a hat. It holds something heavier. I can tell by the way she carries it to the car, or maybe it just seems heavy because my father has not been able to buy the plow he needed. The holes echo out across the fields.

That night, after the dishes are cleared of venison soup and the table wiped of spilled milk, Mom calls me and my brothers, and even my sister Marijo toddles in. My mother's voice is scissor sharp. Now she wants whatever must be done to be done quickly. As she thuds the hatbox down, the old box knows it is done, the yellow glued-together seam splits apart, and buttons burst out from the hatbox, spilling a scattered river of dark stars, white moons and flat suns, a too-strange night sky spread on the oak table. A few skitter to the floor. My brothers scramble for treasure.

In our house, buttons hold small round answers to the plain questions that pop off shirts and pants.

How did you lose another button? Sigh, sigh.

In our house, buttons are little monies like coins, but they close the holes. A button slips through the buttonhole and holds two parts together. Buttons get cut from old shirts to use on not-quite-as-old shirts—so we don't have to buy a new shirt. When we lose a button, she looks for a close match in the button basket. She picks out the button, sews it in place, threading in and out of the holes, and the shirt gets worn until it too has holes.

In our house, the buttons living in our basket are gray, black, or white, or with little swirls like milk in coffee. They are round with two or four tiny holes in the center. Plain as a plowed field.

But this. We pick up the buttons. We gather our hands around them, cupping the mounds as though they were living animals. It makes us happy, this much abundance. We breathe in like clouds before storm. These are from another world, from outer space—like the comic book aliens these buttons, spaceship equipment. And not all of these buttons are round. One button, close to my fingertips, a triangle shining with tiny black sparkles around the edge. In the center, a silver eye. I stare at it. It stares back. Then I see another. Two.

"Are these really buttons?" I put them side by side. Both eyes look at me.

My mother sees the two. "See if you can find more like that."

Is she too from another world?

But I am caught in this rare too-muchness to wonder, already picking up a round red button with gold swirling on its surface, then a tiny one that sparkles with a single rhinestone. Then my fingers stumble onto another silver eyed. A triangle of eyes. A trinity. Like in church, like God? My brother finds four green buttons shaped like tiny birds. Now it's a game. Now we are putting like with like. Matching. While we hunt, my mother cuts cooking string and threads the alike ones together so they make bracelets, all the same on one string.

She sighs, watching us, telling us when she sees a match that we missed. When the boys drop them, she says, "Don't you lose any."

"Are we going to put them on our clothes?" For a moment, I'm so happy I could fly.

She huffs, answers the real question. "These are fancy clothes buttons."

The real answer: we don't have fancy clothes.

Then why is she putting them together like this? If she will not use them? I see her linger over the white pearls. She fingers each before stringing it. I remember a little sweater with pearl buttons she used to wear for church, but baby Patti spit up on it so many times, she couldn't get it clean. Did my mother like these buttons? Would she keep them?

"You could use that for church coat?" I say. Church coat has a top button missing that she covers with a winter scarf.

"Too uppity. And these aren't the right size anyway. Need something bigger for the hole of the button." The button must match the hole. Things must fit inside each other. But I can see her thinking about a button for church coat. She likes this idea.

My brothers get bored when the easy sets are all collected and they have to hunt harder. They drift away to make forts with the old Lincoln Logs. I would like to do that too, but because my brothers have gone, I can't. Then Mom leaves the table to put Marijo to bed, to check on the baby. I stay with the buttons. I keep trying to find the matching ones. For some sets, we have only two, but for some we have many strung, little circled nests.

Have I ever seen more of anything so pretty? More like pieces of story. Because that is what I see begin to rise in these clusters: yellowed pearls, military metal, suggesting dreams of who wore lace and who a uniform, all of it starting to rise in my rogue childhood mind.

She comes back with used envelopes and drops each string of button sets into a separate envelope, crosses out the old addresses, and writes on the outside of the envelope the color and size and number.

"Can I have the . . . ?" I ask, reaching for the red and gold swirly ones. A dancer's button.

"No." Her voice cuts, too firm to argue. "I'm going to sell them."

"Sell them?" I finger a brown one like a dried leaf.

"Someone will pay good money."

The river rises. Rises. She is going to sell the stories that are spreading out now on the table like a pool of spilled water. I will never see them again. I want to beg, but the river runs hard. The holes are deep.

We are almost done. She points to the pile of odd ones that have no matches. "These probably aren't worth anything—no one wants a single button. Take one. The rest go in our basket. We'll get some use."

I paw through the ordinary ones looking for one I like, and here, mystery, wonder, a half thing, not half a disk, but half like half a quail egg, or a tiny blue egg cut straight across the middle, shot with slivers of light like clouds in the dark, like if I could see even more of the pieced-together picture of the world from science class, it would look like this. It's heavy and the hole for the thread is on the underside, hidden, a tiny circlet of metal—so the top is a place un-interrupted. I lift it and hold it out to her to ask. She is surprised. She has not seen this button. But she doesn't see what I am asking. She remembers the church coat.

"Well," she says with a small smile as she seals and labels the last envelope. "It doesn't match anything else, so it's perfect for that top button." Make it useful. Fill where the cold comes in. Close the hole. My fingers touch hers as I hand off the button. She is smiling, my mother who does not smile very much, is smiling, warm in the ever-cool farmhouse.

"What is the...?" I ask, knowing there is a name for this moment.

"That's a sphere, or rather half of it. If there were two, you'd have a whole. Like the earth." She looks pointedly at me. "But then it couldn't close the hole and you'd be cold."

She hates the cold.

Then her little sharp breath cuts the world apart again, and she reaches into the pile, seeing what I have missed. A match, the other half world. She puts them together.

"A pair we can sell."

No half world for my own. No closing the church coat for her.

She runs the strong thread through the metal loops, ties them with string so tightly that these half worlds cling to each other. The science class picture completes its curve of earth. I see it at last. We are not a disk floating in place, edged by ocean or space. We were meant to be whole, half spheres tied by string and metal, rounded to each other. But still, the seam, the empty place where they divide. The sphere is complete, but the thread that holds them can be broken. The world holds together, the worlds could just as easily be sheared apart.

MELONS

After Dad's death, my first goal is to minimize what is required of an eldest daughter. Do just enough so I don't get accused of neglect. Help, along with my siblings, to keep her safe. That's really all that's required, right? What I don't anticipate is the role of memory, how returning to meet even these minimal requirements will invite the past to appear suddenly from its corner, to brush against my legs, a living creature insisting on being fed, begging for meaning.

Now, on the last days of my summer break from teaching, I kiss my beloved David goodbye and drive south for a hundred miles along the west coast of Michigan from Traverse City to my mom's home on the Pentwater River in Oceana County. I've been driving these miles once a week since Dad died, miles to my parents' home, a plain blue two-bedroom ranch perched on a bluff over the river where she has lived with and without help. The *with and without help* is the problem. She's now racked up a history, "letting go" two of the three helpers we have hired. The third one quit, saying, "She doesn't want me here." Got that right.

What shouldn't be hard, getting help for her, is turning into Mount Everest. Despite a public sociability that would put TV personas to shame, despite her grace and generosity to her community, she doesn't like "strangers" in her house. She doesn't want anyone (except family of course) touching anything in it, from bathroom to basement, from closet to kitchen. Her papers, mail, dishes, and living room are off limits. Even food is an issue: food that had once been her forte.

For lunch, I am tackling a melon molded at the blossom end, and from the look, she's taken a whack at it with a carving knife, maybe several times; cuts seep peach-colored juice like sunny blood. With her arthritic hands, how did she wield a carving knife? It takes my breath.

She wobbles into the kitchen, tapping her cane, leans near me. Set at an angle, her cane slips. She catches herself. I catch my breath, tell myself not to shout. But why can't she use her walker in the kitchen, where this slippery linoleum invites a fall? I imagine the fall, her crumpled on the floor, open refrigerator door spilling cold air on her shattered bones as she moans alone for hours. She has severe arthritis in her back and spinal stenosis, a degenerative condition that worsens as one ages, but she refuses the walker unless the walks ice up. She insists only on her cane, a cane that wouldn't support a paper doll.

Last week, she dismissed a woman assigned from Good Shepherd Care, an organization that helps homebound folks. She's been alone since, and the kitchen looks it. It smells old. The soup in a cold pan on the stove has grown a beard. The melon has pocks of gray— is any of it good? I cut it in half.

She has just told me to *leave her alone*, that she is doing *just fine*, and I have reminded her that last week, that trip to the emergency room landed her in the hospital for the night, and now with everyone headed back to school and fall harvests coming on, we are at a crisis.

She announces firmly, "I did not go to the ER." She's seems to be thinking hard, "It was just an appointment." Denial again. Or perhaps simple grief—not that grief is ever simple—or is it . . . confusion? I study her face; she won't meet my eyes.

One half of the melon looks decent. Enough for a lunch snack. When did she last eat? Though burned crumbs pepper the sink, I don't know if she had a real breakfast.

Her cane bumps my legs. She studies the melon, pokes the bad half. "Don't throw that away. I can eat it."

Why does she have to be in this small kitchen?

Oh, it's her kitchen.

"Mom, it's gone rotten on that side." On which side, mine or hers?

"I can eat it."

"It's fermenting."

"Maybe that's why I want it." What?

"You'll get drunk." Trying to be funny.

"Maybe that's why I want it." She doesn't like to be drunk.

Then, in her all-caps voice, "I'll be fine."

How many times has she said she'll *be fine*, but like the melon, something goes bad. She falls or she can't find her checkbook or she's awake in the middle of the night and calls random people in a panic.

"How will you get around?" I ask.

"I can drive."

"Drive where?" It's sixteen miles to Hart, the main town nearby, four to our village of Crystal Valley, seven to the home farm. One neighbor tells us she drives like a bat out of hell. Another says, *You just never know when she's going to stop in the middle.* I abandon the car question, go for the throat, "Mom, it might not be safe for you to live alone."

"I'll get a dog." Get a dog?

"It will protect me."

That's what she fears? A break in? "Not what I meant. You can barely walk. What if you fall?" The old soup makes me nauseous.

"Then I fall. It's my life to fall." She likes that she has said this. She's got that *so there* look on her face.

I want to shout, *What about the rest of us?* What about the worry and expense and the time we take off work and the recovery if you break a hip? What about five adult children in a tizzy of psychic uncertainty, management crisis, and yes, damned right, sleep deprivation. Dad's death has spun us all into a vortex of sorrow none of us would have believed.

I take a breath. "Just out of curiosity, how will you take care of a dog?"

"Oh, dogs are no trouble." Until it chews the remote of your recliner. Until it needs walking. Oh God, she'd let it run wild.

Before this escalates, I try a different tack.

"Mom, you already get so lonely. You call Jackie at night." Jackie's my sister-in-law, my brother Rick's wife, a favorite of Mom's. Jackie's been good about it, but we know.

"A dog would keep me company. Besides, I'm going to get a job."

She's eighty-nine; I don't bring this up. "Where are you going to get a job?"

"I'll go back to nursing."

"It's been fifty years."

"Like riding a bike, not something you forget." Like I'm an idiot.

It's useless to mention that nursing may have changed, or that I found a week's worth of mail in the box, that she's not eating right, that the neighbors are calling. My sister Marijo and I have found her in her chair, staring into space, overwhelmed with the simple task of getting up, trapped in what I thought was a chamber of grief, but then, the chair smelled of urine. We can't seem to talk, we can't seem to move from this place.

How did we get to this? The question provokes an answer in memory, something I have been trying to avoid for weeks and have found it impossible; it wakes me, shakes me, still nips and gnaws at me, that point or points where the thin threads of memory that held parts of our world together finally frayed and broke. Back then.

The easy answer would be this: I was a child of will and she was the mother of no. Listen.

No.

NO.

Nooooooo.

Nonononononono.

Nope.

Noooooooouhuhuhuhuh.

No, you don't.

NONONONO.

NO, no, NO, no, NOOOO.

Noyoucan't.

Noyouaren't.

Uhuhuhuh!

Think of it: combinations, intonations, articulations of that one-syllable word turned to a river the length of the Mississippi. If she went for synonyms, there rose a universe of psychic forbiddens. She could say no with grace and with a fierce, paralyzing anger. She could say no in silence. She could say no with a set of her jaw. She could even say no without saying no. She could say no under circumstances when saying yes would have been beneficial to her.

But now, with Dad gone, the pattern shifts. It's not something I welcome. It scares the shit out of me. Memory interrupts, random but active, attached to a grief she and I and our entire family share but do not easily express. I am cutting a melon, washing a pan, driving, and it rises, clear as a clean window, clear as a mirror. Here, here. Random, fierce, disordered memories. They come: first, the farm, the earliest shards rise from the bedrock of the farm where I grew up. Those memories.

Here's one. A small cave, no, not a cave but a hollowed-out place on slope, a root cellar Dad built for her to store winter vegetables. She sent me out there for cabbage, carrots, but I was afraid of it, afraid of the dark with its lumpy sacks and bushels, and the smell. I wouldn't reach in, would go back to the house, tell her they were rotten. She didn't believe me. *Go back*, she said.

Can't Tom or Rick?

No, you go. She insists. And I do. Into the dark. Then and now. Trying to figure out what happened. The scent of dank soil, the scent of vegetables gone soft. The scent of earth we share.

Now, in her kitchen, and in all the unexpected places along the roads, memory is an insistence I am unable to resist. Trapped by Dad's absence, by loss, memory lures me in, the scent of old soup, of chilled apples, of things fresh picked or rotting, and memory keeps offering up things I had resisted, even as I still resist. I pour the soup down the sink, try to remove the scent of it, but it stays and stays.

There's a condition called broken heart syndrome—it's real. The medical term for it is takotsubo, a Japanese word describing how fisher folk catch octopus by means of a small entrapping jar—the tangle of octopus climbs in and can't get back out. Physiologically: what happens inside the heart, the left ventricle swells. No killing heart attack, just the pain. The heart can heal from takotsubo, but it takes time. It can debilitate the victim for months, sometimes years. To me, it's all metaphor. A chamber of grief, a trap of grief. If you loved my father, as I did, as she did, as we did, this is the kind of grief you have. Our whole family is entrapped in this hollow chamber, but hers is unique; hers is the soft heart of body caught in a hard shell of defiance.

The octopus never believes it is trapped; it thinks it is protected.

This is what's happening, this grief that traps, made of the clay of our pasts, is slowly cracking open.

And me? I had twisted a particular narrative into place, and I intended to stay in the story I had chosen. I scrub the pot clean of other possibilities. I turn to the melon.

After all the nos, the no-ing that went on for years of my childhood, there came the second stage. When she could no longer control what I did, could no longer make me do what she wanted me to do with one word, when she saw how pointless no had become, she changed her tack.

I'm going to the prom, hayride, picnic.

Just don't be stupid.

I'm going to Grand Rapids, to the mall, with my boyfriend.

Just don't wreck the car.

I'm going to the beach.

Just don't show off like something cheap. (That was the worst, the cheap part.)

I'm going to Pizza Hut.

Just don't spend too much money.

I'm going, I'm going, I'm going.

Just don't, just don't, just don't.

What I thought these statements meant: *Stay here. Stay and take pleasure in my company. Stay and do some work with me, and take pride in that. Be like me.* I could not do it. I seemed predestined to explore every single thing she feared. It would not make my life easy; it would make hers miserable.

Now, with her cane, she slams the fridge door behind me.

It's not that she doesn't feel grief; she does, and more deeply than I can imagine. Sometimes I catch her at a softhearted moment, her various guards down, and she gives over, tells me how much she misses him. We sit, she in her chair, me on the ottoman, and we cry. It's comforting until I try to lead her back to what will happen next. A decision, I keep asking for a decision. *Mom, what will you do this winter?* Winter in Michigan. Winter in Oceana County—the county on the lake where the storms hustle over the waters, wraiths turning to solid tons of snow, dumping it all in that long driveway. The decision we (her five adult children) want is not the one she makes. She says she wants to live alone, here on a lonely highway above the North Branch of the Pentwater River, miles from a dying village where the only thing open after five o'clock is the local bar. But she announces over and over: it's her decision. *You don't know anything. I can do this.*

We're trying, Mom.

Are we?

We have been trying *something* all through this long hot summer. After she fired the day help, we hired a night person, thinking maybe that would buy us a good night's sleep, but Mom complained, *We pay her to sleep here?* She made *that woman* coffee, told her not to come back. I set up a schedule with the family. Days and nights we could stay with her, a rotation. My brother Tom puts a stop to that. *We have our hands full here.* My brothers' wives have their own aging mothers and fathers, did I forget that? And the farm, always the farm. We are farmers in a farming county. The farms are living gods, radiating their own set of demands, running their commandments under the daily all.

Hers is a crisis we have to solve before I return to my own world, Interlochen Arts Academy, two hours north, where I also chair a department, have enough administrative duties to sink a ship. Not to mention my own home. My dear husband, David, though patient to a fault, is on his own through this. Marijo and I have talked. Marijo lives near enough to be a participant in Mom's life, but she works too, and her relationship with Mom is more fraught than mine though for different reasons. And yet, once a week, she is spending a day with Mom, and once a week, the miles tug me toward her house on the river, toward the unknowing of us, as though I were homing inevitably toward some other knowing. But what?

Hoping some flavor remains, I cut melon into slices, segment moon-shaped pieces, and slice off the rind. "Mom, we're wondering if you might want to tour Cherry Blossom Manor." Cherry Blossom Manor is not a manor. It's a sprawling, industry-style home, a cross between assisted living and adult foster care. It has a good reputation, is clean and safe, and it's in our hometown, Hart, only sixteen miles away.

I step back, look at her with what I hope is a friendly suggestion expression. I forget I am holding a knife. I can tell, if she could swing that cane at me, she would do so with gusto. But she's swaying, an old birch in wind, and suddenly she plunks down on the stool. I know what she's thinking. It's been with us all these weeks. That knife-like question. *Why can't I live with one of you?* A question designed to pierce a chamber of the heart, transform it into a weeping melon.

I put down the blade. Turn to the fridge, open the door. Toward the back. *Oh God, another melon. She bought two?*

Other guilts rise in the scent of spoiled fruit. Here are three. My mother was primary caretaker for our family's elders. My mother took into our farmhouse my father's mother, Josephine; then her own mother, Julia; and my father's invalid sister, Mary—in our

small farmhouse—with seven already there. Sometimes one, sometimes all three elders at once. We lived with them; they with us. We
grew up as they grew old. It might have looked like the Waltons
from the outside, but it was not idyllic. It was crowded; it was work
without joy; it created expectations in her that we could not meet.
How do you keep up with laundry, with meals, with a house, with
fields, and a husband who needed sometimes to work off the farm
to keep it going? She needed outside help but could never ask, never
felt she could hire, so we were her staff for what little we, no I, was
worth. It wasn't much, what with defiance running through me like
light.

Now, she wanted us to do the same for her. That was the bargain
she had struck three times, with three elders' lives, maybe even with
her trinity-ridden God. She'd paid forward, done a good daughter's duty, and now karma should be balanced. Having set the bar so
high, she expected her own daughters to step up.

My own karma doesn't give a shit.

Her cane taps the linoleum.

I pull my head out of the fridge. "Mom, what about this other
melon?"

The other melon. My own karma turns its back.

Yes was also in her being. She was really a yes mom in many ways,
but we had to say it to her. Yes, I'll go to church, learn to sew, do
dishes, hoe the beans. Yes to being pleasant and yes to serving others. All good stuff to expect for a mom of her time, but she was out
of her league when it came to me, her eldest. I said yes to most of
the teaching, most public behaviors. I understood she was trying to
knead me into something good, but I could not say yes to her need-
ing me. I could only echo her no.

Now I know that yes also included opportunity. Because I was
the first, and she was, in her own way, determined to do right by
me. So though I'd been a wild child—we'd managed early on. There
had been tenderness and what I now know was good upbringing.
There were years of, if not rapport, at least care. But then the teen
years of wrestled rebellion that should have, once done, drawn us

closer instead wedged us apart like a maul breaks the log. When it became clear I should go to college, not because I was gifted, but because they didn't know what else to do with me, I did not choose Michigan State University—the agricultural college of my parents' loyalty. Instead, I chose Grand Valley State, a small liberal arts college with a reputation for left-wing politics. And somewhere in those years, I began to lie. I was not good at it, was often caught, but it got me out from under the no-ing. Is that when she and I began to set ourselves as opposite poles on a planet that should have been made of affection? Even love? We were not friends; rather, we were a broken connection. Yes and no, no and yes, two halves of a fractured world. But now, as these days close in on the end of this summer the color of sorrow, memory oh memory again, interferes with the pattern, frays to a ragged edge I can finger. Go back, go back and see what's there.

First, my leaving. The loudest no of all. My own. Not how you might think.

Two years into college. We are standing in the badly carpeted lobby of that long-ago college apartment building. I have just paid a late-rent fee. I'm always late—not being responsible, another way of my saying no. She has driven the two plus hours from home in Hart to the center of the state, Grand Valley's campus, to check on me, which she does, often without warning—and usually because I have not called her, and she wants to know why, especially now that my boyfriend and I, a boy she considers a saint, are on rocky ground.

She's sitting in a hard vinyl chair. Light from a window falls on her nearly white hair. I'm standing. I have something to say to her.

"Mom," I take a breath. "I want to apply for the Junior Year Abroad program."

"What's that?" She looks up, caution already turning sour in her mouth.

"It's a junior year with a twist." Twist is perhaps not the appropriate word. "They take four sophomores in good standing, and you study in another country."

"Like Canada?"

"I'd leave in September."

"Where?" Her voice is escalating; mine going quieter.

"Overseas." Tension like old gum. "I'll work all summer. I'll cover the extra cost."

"No." The word is the snap of the slingshot in thin air.

"I might not get it. Abroad programs are competitive."

"You are not applying for any program that takes you that far away." Her voice.

"I already did." Silence like still water before the stone hits it.

Then she is on her feet, in my face, "Who do you think you are? Pulling a stunt like that without talking to your father or me."

I'm not anybody, Mom, but I'm going to Europe. To England, to study for a year, to change the direction of my life. To be lonely and maybe just maybe to learn what I'm missing, some knowledge about life away from you.

I could speak none of this. I knew only this much: this was my yes to myself. This was me crossing an ocean to make sure I meant it. Yes, I would miss the family, my sisters and brothers more than I could say, and sometimes I would cry for them, from lonesomeness for my family, our farm, but I would not have to bear her no. And I wanted . . . something more.

But "no" came to represent a pattern that she could see and I could see too, but we would not, could not, break it. "No" was her code: *Be her model child. Do what she asked.* That's all I heard for the longest time. My no to her was the only way I could break up with her. My no was leaving her country, not the United States, but the country of Mother. The country of No. All that teen drama, all those shouting matches—what I fail to acknowledge is that in the end they gave me permission to get on a plane and fly away. When Dad said yes, she stopped arguing, she gave in.

When did I realize I'd have to come home?

Now I was nearing sixty, and she was nearing ninety. No changing now, not this late in the game. Besides, who wanted to change— we'd been at stalemate for so long it felt like who we were. De- cades ran rampant between that day I announced I was leaving and

Dad's dying. In that time: Three degrees—one of which she disapproved (*Creative writing?* What will you do with that?). Three men—all of whom she disapproved (Can't you find a *Catholic?*). Two marriages—one for which she prophesied doom on the day she met him (That's who you want to spend *your life* with?). She was right on that, but I would never admit it. It ended in shambles. My marriage to David had softened her—*a quiet man, a good man*, but I could read subtext like she could read the weather—I was still the only divorcée in the family. And then, he was Presbyterian.

But each time I drive the two hours from my house near Traverse City to hers near Crystal Valley, our lives, carved out of the debris of leavings, rise up in those shards of memory, sharp pieces of clay. Over time she had claimed she was proud of me, though we both knew I was not what she had hoped I would be. I'm not living in home country, Oceana County, but far enough away to make visits downright inconvenient. I'm not attentive to the family or the farm, not a practicing Catholic, not a tidy cook. I don't care about housekeeping, don't sew anymore, don't—this one is hardest of all for her—*want children*. With all this history rising up through the miles, by the time I arrive at her house, I'm on the defensive before a word is said.

But now my sisters and I are learning something else. While I was off teaching, traveling, and writing for all those years, Dad had covered for her, tucked a blanket of assurances over her growing disabilities. Now we were seeing it lifted: her forgetting what was in the refrigerator, on the stove, in the cupboards was the smallest symptom. Bathing, another. When we talked her into a bath, we found she couldn't lift herself in and out—her own dead weight, so to speak. The shower—a nightmare of resistance. Then, the incontinence—all that slow leaking, which she, apparently, could not smell. I could see now that he had hid more than that: also, her shifting mental landscape. We'd always known her physical frailty and we knew how it coupled with her fight, but now her reactions—and her shrillness—were differently inspired. Not only did the usual irritations set her off, but her temper was unpredictable, unprovoked, and sometimes not based on facts. It's there now: her whip-sharp tongue rises to the surface and strikes right there in the kitchen, "Don't you dare touch that melon." She stands up, a rocket taking off.

Okay Mom, *hands off.*

If the hygiene issue weren't enough, her location was. Remote and rural. To make a cell call, I position myself in the ditch at the end of a driveway so long it passes for a hike—just to pick up one bar—and that doesn't always connect. Then the architecture. You'd think a simple ranch-style house would be navigable, but there were stairs to the garage, stairs to the basement, stairs to the front garden, stairs down to the river—an elder's dance with injury. Then, finances: car, bills, maintenance, taxes. What had once seemed second nature to her capable mind was now a snow-slope of envelopes avalanching off the side table. Now, she called neighbors in the night, lost important papers, tried to drive but forgot where. We sisters had ransacked options, and it always returned to the revelation of our father's death: Mom needed twenty-four-hour care. Preferably in her home. Or one of ours. Or someplace else. That one was unthinkable. Or was it?

I hate every moment of this.

Because I'm thinking it right there in her kitchen: that *someplace else.* Someplace else is the dilemma of we twenty-first-century boomers. Home? Almost every woman had a job outside the home. Our families depended on both spouses working. An entire culture dependent on two incomes. How did that work when someone needed care?

After the failure of the outside help, my sisters and I talked about giving up our jobs and living with her in her home. But who relieved us? And how? Who would come and let us go to our husbands, our families? Did Marijo and I both quit our jobs and alternate? Besides teaching, my writing career was demanding and growing. I wanted to respond flexibly to requests from libraries and conferences, to speak about the books I had written. And to write. What if I did take Mom to my own home—how deep would her loneliness be there, where she knew no one and no one knew her? Because I knew this: I wouldn't give up my writing for her; it had been too hard won, coming from a family where I was the first one to finish a four-year degree, a master's, a book, then three. I would not choose the resulting bitterness.

That's the daughter I was.

No easier for Marijo. Marijo had a demanding job in the social services sector. If Marijo took Mom into her home—Mom would at least be in Hart, our hometown, but that meant that Marijo would have to quit working. She was already helping to support a grandchild, and her job with special needs adults was challenging and important, though also physically and psychically exhausting—and to be honest, her relationship with Mom had its own set of dark corners. Further, if Marijo took in Mom and tried to keep working even part-time, then Marijo's dear husband, John, whose in-home office could be a rally of phone calls and run-outs, would also have to contend with Mom. Even part-time, it wasn't viable for them.

Then there was Pat, youngest daughter and the child warmest with Mom but farthest away in distance. Pat, my Colorado mountain sister whose family existed in those altitudes, those snow-laden mountainsides. There she had a yoga practice and helped with Duane's business. Though she felt worse than any of us about the distance, the most she could offer was a week or two a couple times a year—which was a lot, considering. Our brothers and their wives, Tom with Jill, Rick with Jackie, faced similar questions with their other sets of parents. Maybe different people could have found a way, but in the end, it was our own rotten melon.

I close Mom's fridge on the second melon, return to salvaging the first one, and cut the wine-scented pieces off the rind. I hand her the bowl. We all love to eat with our fingers, and anything that doesn't demand a fork, we will pick at. She lifts a piece up with her fingers. She tastes, "Just the way Dad likes it," she says.

Dad, oh Dad. Dad's not here. But there was a day, right there in childhood somewhere. He had brought home melons, half a dozen small soft melons from a farm stand somewhere, and there at summer's end with all of us gathered on the back porch, we had cut them in half and ladled in scoops of ice cream and ate them in the long-angled heat. It was joyous; it was generous in a way that was rare in the household.

I study the fibery cluster in the bowl, peach-faded, running with age. When I taste, the flavor is flat. I do what we all do to flavorless fruit, we farm families. I sprinkle salt on the melon, and tasting only salt, I speak the words at last. "Mom, I can stay until tomorrow. Then I gotta start teaching. Let's go and tour the Manor in the morning. Just to research some options."

I am lying through my teeth.

My mother stomps her cane, a sure sign she's about to use it for something other than balance. Then she sinks for the second time onto the kitchen stool. The sigh is the sigh of a saint, a martyr, a no-choice, *fuck-this* sigh—though she would never say that. I stand in her kitchen light, and I know—we are creatures trapped in the clay vessel, caught in a long silence of no. I've perfected my end of the no and don't intend to change. I will not take her.

And then she nods.

This is not how it should go. This is exactly how it's going. She has offered her yes, a grudging, helpless yes.

My hands drip with melon.

DENIAL AND IGNORANCE:
A SUMMARY

During the tour of the Manor, she huffed and humphed, but publicly she smiled at all the right people as only she could. As we left, she whispered, "Too many Methodists," and demanded to go home. Two falls and many frantic phone calls later, Marijo and I helped her move to the Manor, despite the Methodists. Despite assurances from the folks at the home that she would be paired with "someone nice," she hated her roommate, a helmet-haired elder who had been alone long enough to become territorial as a dragon. Marijo, bless her, finally finagled Mom another room, a larger space with a bedridden roommate on oxygen who rang a bell for assistance every ten minutes. Mom played the public martyr about that damned bell, silent and pissed, but then finally did complain. The woman was scolded, a "talking to" resulted, but then Mom felt terrible. Finally, the unthinkable. The roommate up and died. I thought selfishly: *Well, Mom will feel more independent, settled in a room of her own. Hell, she'll decorate.* She loved decorating. Froufrou galore.

How little I know.

One Saturday, I arrive, enter Mom's room to find all of her clothes and that decor stacked on the bed. She putters at her dresser, swaying against her cane. "I don't know why you girls brought so much stuff from home. Now I have to take it all back."

"Mom, what are you doing?" I'm staring at three piles of knee-high nylon stockings.

"Where's my suitcase?"

"At Marijo's."

"What's it doing there?" Her voice winding like a top.

"Why are you packing?" I ask.

"To go home." I can feel the coils tightening. Any minute she will fly into the air like an angry hornet. Or is that me? I pick up half a dozen knee-high stockings. Could I throw them? Wouldn't hurt her but the gesture would hold our old drama. She wobbles, a blue-green chiffon scarf trailing from her hands—her colors slipping to the floor. The silence between us: question and answer, accusation and defense. Blue and green. I watch her fingering the chiffon dream of home. I cannot bear what needs to be said.

"Mom, you know how hard winter is out there. Maybe in the spring . . ."

Her face crumples and she sinks into her chair—is resignation always about sitting down? I lift the chiffon and fold it into a tiny square. She stares out the window at the bird feeder where no birds feed. I repack her dresser, all the knee-highs.

She falls asleep in her chair. I remember that Grandma Julia used to do that too, fall asleep in the chair by our front window. It was a way of shutting out the world. For a moment, their images overlap, Mom and Grandma, but then it comes to me. Grandma was in our home.

Mom does not wake when I kiss her goodbye. What kind of daughter leaves her mother where she is so unhappy?

Ignorance shows up. Marijo and I are ill equipped to understand the financials of Mom's care. Neither of us has ever paid much attention to the particulars of elder expenses. How do we handle the insurance? What's the difference between Medicare and supplemental Plan A? B? N? Are there survivor benefits for Dad's having served in World War II? What does Mom's small trust hold? How much money? How much money? How much money?

Why does she have so many pairs of sheer knee-highs?

Marijo and I are often sleepless, trying to figure out forms and procedures, not to mention how our hearts ache with uncertainty and the outright fear that we will make an irrevocable mistake because we have little idea what we are doing. We spend precious mornings on the phone, waving our hands in the air, taking illegible notes, mouthing a whole new vocabulary. I always feel as though I'm asking the wrong questions. One of the wrong questions is about her mind. She is physically challenged, yes, but the other signs: forgetting, sudden anger, losing the calendar of her mind.

Hygiene.

How could it be that a woman who was a fanatic nurse, who had taught us to keep meticulously clean, now resisted water like an old cat. There had been challenges to cleanliness in our house, our lives on a farm, but she had always fought the dirt war, wrestling it to the ground like it was her superpower.

Even during harvests, when no one had an iota of extra energy for baths or even much washing up, and we all traipsed in from the field caked with dust and grime so thick we could write our names on our skin, she would use what means she had. She fed us hastily, piled us into the old station wagon, drove the back roads to School Section Lake, and there in the shallows, away from others, she plunked us down, bar soap hidden in her palm, and washed us. We played in those waters, resurrecting spirit and skin, until we would sleep so deeply she feared we'd never wake. This was not the mother of No, but the mother who wanted us clean to the point where she'd risk shaming herself at a public beach, albeit a remote one.

During my visits to her now, as these memories accumulate, I find myself trembling unexpectedly: What if she is not the mother I had decided I knew? What if she was not that angry, stubborn, critical, directive, and utterly committed mother on which I had based an entire narrative? I cannot imagine—and this is hard—not feeling annoyed with her. Not defining myself in contrast with her.

But here is memory of water, here is a small lake with a beach to run across, here are her hands splashing us, refreshing the skin of childhood, wiping it clean.

She's not settling in at the Manor. Whereas she was rarely happy in her little house, now she's on the other side of miserable. She contracts a serious upper respiratory infection, and in a chronic state of low-grade fever, cries or lashes out every time I see her. She hates that we've "abandoned" her at the Manor, she's grief-stricken that Dad is dead, appalled that she has no control, and wants to go home to the river. But another word is ringing, entering consciousness, on the edge of being spoken: it flickers with dull light, soft and barely audible. That other word.

Midwinter, an angel. Marijo's daughter, Brooke, my beautiful beloved niece, has left her boyfriend and is coming home. She needs a quiet place, needs to make some money, and needs a new purpose. Could Brooke be the means to bring Mom home, back to the River House? Would Brooke live at Mom's house with her, see that things were ... safe, taken care of? Marijo asks; Brooke is willing. Mom is ecstatic, Marijo and I, drenched in relief.

And just like that, denial moves in, covering up the word we almost heard.

We make arrangements, breathing our hopeful fantasies. Sure, we can pay Brooke; sure, we can finish the basement of Mom's house—should have been done years ago. Sure, make an apartment there; sure, Brooke can get a job for a few hours every day; sure, *anything, Brooke, anything*, just come. Save us.

During one visit, I catch our brother Tom on his way to the farm. He stops to talk, leans out of his truck window. I share the good news. He lifts his cap to scratch his head, "Can Brooke handle it?"

"She's a grown-up." I'm standing next to the truck window, but we stare out at the fields as farmers do.

"You know how she is." He wipes his forehead, smearing dust on his thinking parts.

"Brooke?"

"Brooke's fine! Great in fact." He looks at me pointedly. "*I mean Mom*. You know how Mom gets."

Of course, I know how Mom gets. But Mom adored Brooke. They would have a love fest. Brooke, the benevolent rescuer. Mom, the adoring elder.

"It won't be . . . easy," Tom warns.

"It will be fine." I think. The field is pocked with weeds.

Tom sighs, nods, puts the truck in gear, returns to his fields. I repeat, as though repeating could make it so: *This will work, this will work.* Denial lurks in the ditch.

Brooke moved in and, bless her heart, lasted three whole months.

Tom had been correct. We had denied day-to-day life with Mom. How for Mom, nothing was ever as right as it might be, nothing was ever without regret or improvement or some measure of strident worry. I know these are the ways of many mothers. But I wondered if other mothers expressed it as our mother did. For example, she did not throw things, never that dramatic, but instead, slammed them, so if one were sensitive, one could decipher the degree of her annoyance by the quality of the slam. She had a knack. Slamming was universal language. Plates, doors, cupboards, a whole monologue of complaint and irritation in one quick bang.

Then there was the consistency issue. Even as Mom told Brooke how grateful she was for her help, she would scold her for taking too many showers, for leaving on a stray light, for her cat scratching the woodwork. Mom would dive into Brooke's frittata like she'd never eaten before and simultaneously play guilt like a high-strung violinist—*too much food*. Brooke had taken that part-time waitressing job in the afternoons, times when, even though Mom usually took long naps, she woke worried: Brooke was her kid again, all of her kids, every kid in the world, and here Mom was, *waiting up again*, she said—never mind it was midafternoon. And then Mom was tight as a clingstone peach to the pit, did I say that? *Why should I pay for her to work somewhere else?*

I try to explain: *But she's here at night, Mom, and in the morning, you have coffee and breakfast together, and she's a good cook—you get good meals. And laundry and cleaning. And she looks out. And she's always in reach of the phone. And she needs to get away, and you need time ... for your naps.*

Brooke is patient. Brooke is kind. Brooke ... is looking at us, wondering what we got her into. We don't blame her. Mom assures me that she and Brooke are doing just fine. Except that's not what Brooke says. Brooke is realizing our mother is more than a tough cookie. My mother, under her gracious public persona, is as tough as old steak with a cheap sweet-sour reduction.

One night, while Brooke slept in the too-cool unfinished basement that Mom refused to let us refinish despite our promises to Brooke, a storm rolled in off the lake, one of those storms with big wind that accelerated as it moved inland, that went on for a long time with crackling sky and lions'-roar thunder, and woke Mom on the main floor in her bedroom but not Brooke in the quiet bowels of the house. It rained so hard, Mom thought the basement would flood. She crawled from her bed to the basement stairs, calling, and was halfway down the stairs, sliding on her butt, before Brooke woke to her cries, disoriented and alarmed, in that heart-racing fear when one is wakened from deepest sleep. It was a terrible moment for both of them: the basement floor perfectly dry, but thunder crashing and lightning breaking open trees on the river, and Mom stuck on the stairs, suddenly confused and scolding, her shrillness jack-knifing through a stormy dark, and Brooke coming out of a sleep with no patience, fear coursing through her own nervous system.

The practical realization that Marijo and I came to: our hope had been misplaced, a false escape out of hard truth. I felt most terrible for Brooke, who had lived with Mom's despair, with her fearful projections. It had broken their relationship. We hadn't faced honestly what it would mean to live with a grieving and judgmental elder, all this while Brooke was trying to heal from a breakup. This is called, in psychology speak, passive acknowledgment—all the evidence is there and obvious. One senses, one may even know, but one doesn't acknowledge the real. My brother Tom had been right; we knew how Mom could be, and we'd ignored it. And then there was something else Brooke reported, that other word that would continue the practice of passive acknowledgment.

Mom was moving beyond resisting baths.

When Brooke left Mom's house, Marijo and I, both working at our real-life jobs, called Pat. Pat, bless her, flew home from Colorado for a few weeks, through Mom's ninetieth birthday, which we celebrated at Marijo and John's sweet farmhouse with cake, balloons, and little sausages wrapped in gooey dough that Mom likes—pigs in a blanket. About a hundred cards. Many visitors. Mom was, as always in public, welcoming, smiling and warm, but under that charm, no one could refute her sadness. Maybe it was that she couldn't blow out those ninety candles, and the haze of that many candles, once lifted, prophesied what would come.

I don't remember a pinpoint conversation. Maybe there wasn't one. But after that, even Mom was resigned. In May, as asparagus season rose up with its howling demands for harvest, for days of duty in dusty fields, and the fields cried for the care of every farmer in the region, Marijo drove Mom back to the Manor. This time, Marijo opted for a private room, a higher level of care, an aid to monitor meds, the whole damned works. The one hard truth we had come to. Not only were we not going to care for her in our homes, she was not going to live in her own home. She would live at the Manor. We knew that we would blow through the small nest egg that had been my parents' savings, but we also knew this was how it should be used. Three years, maybe four if we cashed in the insurance policy. That small trust that they had assured us was plenty, that held enough that we need not be concerned, just *live your lives*, well, it was not much after all. Mom came from a long-lived family, so like many families with folks this age, we would watch an elderly parent go broke in a place she didn't want to be. The denied question, what we would do when we ran through that nest egg, floated in the future, undefined, blocking a word that floated even beyond that. The word, dementia.

THE WALL

First, we decide to paint the walls of their house. Mom and Dad's retirement house of twenty-five years, the unassuming "dream" house they built when they were my age, where they had lived until the summer Dad passed, has not been painted since they moved in. Paint the walls of the home they built for their go-go years and even their no-go years. Paint the walls of this place from which they believed they would be carried on some assembled-on-the-spot stretchers straight to the plot at the cemetery. Except for the final six days in the CCU at the end, this had proven true for my father. But Mom, always a different story. My mother, and perhaps all of us, had lived with the illusion they'd live forever. Together. Even after the unbelievable, that he died, Mom was determined to keep her part of forever.

Now she's at the Manor, not in this simple home she loved.

The paint is thick with the chill of the house. No one is here with me. What I must do: paint the walls as part of the slow process of cleaning, clearing, and preparing it for a renter so we can make a little more money to extend Mom's stay at the Manor. This time, the bathroom. It's a small room: shower/tub combo, toilet, vanity, linen cupboard, none of it tricked-out for disability. Too-small doors, little commode space. No tub bars, not even mats. An ordinary bathroom. It shouldn't take long, this ordinary-as-their-lives bathroom; it's taken months.

I have come at last to this one extraordinary wall. Marijo has done the harder work, peeling Mom's fanciful wallpaper like wax from skin. But even with Marijo's hearty sanding, they are revealed, all still legible, dozens of signatures. The well-wishers' names in their own hands with an array of implements: crayons, magic markers, pens, pencils; Max, Pauline, Evelyn, Carlene, Adam, Charlie, John, Don, Celeste, even Father Pete—the parish priest, all the friends, cousins, aunts, uncles, nieces, nephews, and neighbor upon neighbor had signed their names on that wall over the commode. Funny lettering by children who now have children. A couple of rude cartoons. The wall, signed during a country housewarming. All those folks signed the wall of a house not yet complete, a house our parents moved into while the walls were still raw and unprimed. If there is a way to understand something of their ilk, it is perhaps through this wall, this house, this river, and the flood.

I am to paint over it all, make every name disappear. Erase history, so I think.

In the early 1980s, my parents had turned our sprawling childhood farmhouse over to my brother Tom and his wife, Jill. Mom and Dad bought this narrow lot, two acres on the horseshoe of the river, looking south. In summer, dappled light through dense undergrowth, river below, a lush stretch for salmon to spawn. The lot proper sat on a bluff anchored by maples, abundant myrtle, and grapevine, a lot that called for something grander than their simple two-bedroom ranch. They could have afforded more, but neither felt they could be uppity—*What would the neighbors think—getting above themselves like that?* Still, unpretentious and modest, it was their dream house. They intended to build as much as possible by themselves—contracting only the mechanics. They were do-it-yourselfers down to their cells, so they bargained with construction workers for Dad's muscle and know-how—and a discount. They would take their time, enjoy this process, the only house they would build for themselves.

My siblings helped, but as far as I was concerned, my parents were on their own that summer they decided to move all their stuff from the farmhouse to an A-frame rental cottage on the river's floodplain just below their own lot. Mom and Dad would live temporarily in this A-frame rental, close to the work site of the dream house. From the A-frame below, the new house was easy to access— just up the bluff. They packed the A-frame with their most precious stuff, preparing to move it when the house was ready.

By the time the flood came, the new house's foundation was blocked in, the walls framed and sided, windows set, roof on, but nothing interior was complete, no interior walls, minimal floors, no plumbing or wiring. Despite their drive, it was taking a long time. They didn't ask me to help; they shouldn't have had to.

But what *was* I doing? By the mideighties, I was living near Traverse City, teaching full-time, directing the school's theater program, directing *Canterbury Tales* at the local playhouse, running my first educational committee on writing across the curriculum, divorcing, testing a new relationship, and trying to figure out if I could be a writer. Full swing. Did I say I was divorcing my first husband? It's true that my parents had tried to be kind to me about the divorce, really, but their shame stung, and I wanted nothing to do with their judgments. The more important thing was that I had decided to become a writer—after all the years of dithering with my first husband's failed artistic dreams, I realized one thing. I was the one who wanted to be an artist, to focus on the creative in language, and it was up to me, only me. That was the bigger reason I kept my distance. I didn't want my mother near this tender new life. That, and the plans for their new house didn't impress me—couldn't they have been a little more creative?

And then, about the new man in my life. When I had told them that we were serious and mentioned in passing that his family was Catholic (never mind he wasn't practicing), they wondered if, no, *she* wondered if I could get an annulment from my first marriage, you know, *If you are that serious, then you could return to the Church, and if it came to that, you could be married in the church. You could take the sacraments. Wouldn't that be nice for a change?*

I lift the brush, laden with paint, and smear the layer on thickly.

When one builds a house, no one counts on a flood. It was, those good Christians would all say later, like the Deluge, like what Noah must have faced. I wasn't there, but I have pieced it together from family accounts, retellings, and research. A late summer 1986 edition of the *Oceana Herald-Journal* claims sixteen inches of rain fell in the first twenty-four hours. Then, the rain kept on keeping on. On the third day, the Hart dam broke, overwhelmed, and sent a cascade of dark water downriver, washing out houses and flooding the plains. These normally open stretches, laced often with cattail meadows or sedgey fens, these spaces that had not been flooded for decades, took the brunt of the surge. The lowlands, hit the worst, spread wide and mean with running current and rose swiftly higher than they had in memory: in some places both banks collapsed as the fattened rivers swirled wildly through the rolling hills and wide river flats of Oceana County, which at last earned its name.

Dreaming their dreams, my parents slept on in that rented A-frame below the bluff and east of their building lot, slept in that tentlike house on the mosquito-ridden grassland that had once been floodplain, the structure built only three feet off fertile ground but set plenty back from shoreline, which was lined by a driveway, running down a berm along the bluff. Mom and Dad had crowded boxes of everything into the small rooms. Their dog, Sasha, lived with them in joy, for the rabbits had inundated the grassy plain and their warrens were hidden in the bluff at the back of this broad field.

Of course, among the boxes of everything, there was family history. Family pictures, albums, sentimentals from letters to birth certificates, all boxed in the living room at the front, in the room facing the river, the room where in the hot summer evenings Mom could sit and sort, planning portrait galleries for her new hallways in the house above. During the day, my parents put in long hours on the house. At night they slept deeply, too tired to address the aches of their midsixties. They were still hearty and driven.

Then came those rains. On and off for days, and then full on. I imagine it happened like this: My folks settled down in the A-frame on a night when the hard percussion on the roof entered their bodies like a drum. Dad kept going to the screen door, swinging it open over the stoop, checking the speeding river. After dark, he turned on the yard light and watched the river break over the banks, watched it creep across the low field, at first slowly, then not. He saw how quickly the ground under their feet became saturated, then covered. First a few inches, then a foot, slowly climbing the front stoop. He made his way out to the car, but water already swirled around the pedals. It wouldn't start. He waded back, kept watching, thinking it would level off. He said later that he should have left then. Sasha scratched to go out, but when they opened the door, water was everywhere, a dark lake, and now scrub debris, old floats, mysterious objects swirled in the light. The dog retreated to the living room, whining.

Then, the power died. They collected flashlights.

One thing about Mom—she is afraid of water. Her version of taking a swim is to wade in to her knees, squat to get her bottom wet, and return to the shore as quickly as possible. Her version of a day at the beach is a series of warnings and shrieks: *not so far out, get back in here, you'll get cramps*, this in reference to some rule about not swimming for three hours after you eat—I swear she confused it with fasting for Holy Communion. So, when the flood hit the top step, almost three feet, Dad knew even before he saw her eyes, even before he heard her rant of contradiction: *What are we still doing here, and don't you expect me to make a move in that water.*

He found rope, tied it to Mom's waist, made her put on a jacket, tied the rope to his own waist, and guided her, as she swore and scolded, *I am not going!* Then off the stoop, down the steps into the murk, into the swollen river. Knowing the little A-frame might at any moment give out in the current swirling around its makeshift foundation, they left everything, even the dog.

Dad said later he could feel the current but found the gravel bottom by feel, because he had big feet. But all that water rippled wraithlike in the dark, erased landmarks, made a rough lake instead of river. If they followed where they thought the driveway should be, they would be on a firmer bed but would have to walk closer to the original shoreline, where the tug and tumbling debris could bump and scrape and take them down.

He pulled Mom into the flood. *You son of a bitch.* He told me later the only other time she'd sworn at him like that, she was in labor for Rick.

In the end, they crossed the back flats, wading through thick black water with flashlights to the wet slope. They crawled directly up the mud-slicked bluff, hanging onto saplings, grass, and roots. They climbed the rugged clay ridge, chilled and soaked to their souls, and then, muddy and bedraggled, reported to the neighbors, Carlene and Adam, who took them in, gave them hot coffee laced with brown liquor. My mother didn't stop scolding my dad, the world, the entire universe, for days.

While the river filled, bloated and obese, the sky raged on with its extravagant, overbearing rain. An entire day passed before the river peaked, and another before it leveled and began to drop. When the current slowed, an upriver neighbor launched a boat and managed to fight the flux to the A-frame cottage, ruined but still anchored, and woke the dog, who was sleeping on top of the refrigerator, having lived on stale bread and potato chips. The water was three-quarters up the walls. The dog saw the boat, apparently its prow nosing in just below the door's header, dived in, and swam to the men, who pulled her in, trembling and happy.

Before the end of the week, the entire community, from barkeeps to pastors, were retelling the story of John and Ruth (and the dog) climbing out of the flood, the launch of a family tale with biblical overtones.

As to that dream house on that higher ground overlooking that rivery horseshoe—though wet, the unfinished structure weathered this hundred-year rain without a leak or shudder. The banks did not give way, the curve of river did not carve out and drop the new structure into the current. It all held. That simple ranch became their strength, salvation, history, and identity in this new phase of their lives. Unassuming as it was, it would mean *this is who and what we are.* We can build a thing to survive a hundred-year rain, an ark in flood. And they would be the survivors who built it, yes, after the fact, but hell, they were here to tell the story. Complete with the pup. The cleanup was brutal.

After the waters receded, Mom returned to the muddy A-frame on the flats and raked through the mess, gleaning what she could, doing laundry at one neighbor's house after another. Oddly, the oldest family albums survived. The tough paper had not disintegrated, and because the albums were boxed, the photos were soaked through but not destroyed. She could pry open the red leather bindings, separate the sheets. The red dye of these sturdy old covers ran through every page, a rust rivering black-and-white prints, ancestors tinged now with sunburn. She clothespinned the grand old portraits of these hard-core, nineteenth-century immigrants on a rigged up clothesline. All my stern grandpas and grandmas, my greats from a hundred years back, streaked and warped, faced the light and wind again at last until they dried and curled, and she could press them with dictionaries and Bibles and reset them in the new plastic-paged album.

But for all the attention to those ancestors, the descendants (my parents) were temporarily homeless, staying here and there in the community, even returning to the farmhouse for a while. The neighbors stepped in, donating and helping with installations and food. But the house my folks had intended to take their time on had to be finished quickly, under the kind of duress that nerved up my mother and left my dad rail thin. The drywall went on without being mudded, one bathroom had running water but no sinks, and they finished a basement only enough to move in a sofa bed. They cooked on a tiny grill, and when they finally moved up to the main floor, they had painted few walls, and certainly not that bathroom. My parents worked the way they had always worked, as though their lives depended on it, and within weeks, the house could bear company.

The party is infamous in family lore, in the way party stories grow in importance as time passes, and who knows now how the bathroom signings started. Joke, ceremony, a way to mark time? Maybe fifty names. Children now grown, elders now gone. Some of the grandkids' names, Zack and Brooke, appear more than once, as though they enjoyed permission to write on a wall and needed to do it twice for the sheer fun. Mom left the names there for two years before she wallpapered. She waited as long as possible to cover the names of the people who had been there for them. That's what Marijo and I have stripped away, the paper that reveals who they were to a community. Beloved.

Mine is not there. I could add it now. My hand hovers.

When I saw her at last after the flood, her hair, salted early in her life, had gone bone white. We hadn't spoken for weeks. She'd made it clear I'd let her down, that I should have been there, that everyone else had come. "They all asked where you were, why you weren't here." Voice cutting through excuses like a boat through water. I probably walked out.

I bring the brush down. Painting the wall takes three coats, even after primer, and even then, the shadow of Brooke's name, with her multipronged E shines through. The last coat of "Dancing on Air" blue rolls over the signatures like a bulldozer, covering the community that I'd had the opportunity to join.

Now, the flood has long receded—and as I paint, so has anger, replaced by a paint that will dry to a hard finish. The names are gone. Only if I look closely can I feel the shadows through layers. Even as this story is being erased, it is not the closure I think it is.

Mom wanted to stay in this simple two-bedroom river house. If she couldn't have her Noah, she wanted her plain ark. What makes any of us deaf to that cry? The simple answer: I considered my life more important than hers. Arrogance wrapped in ambition.

We write our names to feel momentarily immortal, but in the end, our names point only and always toward mortality, to our insignificance. They will be lost, painted over. I can't place my name here now, can't join the community. It's too late for that, better left buried in the debris of some flood long past. And memory, that flickering light, has only just begun its spiral of insistence.

CHEESECAKE

She who fed half the county at her home table wants lunch. Out. "My treat," I say grandly. Today, Open Hearth Grille, and though she's hobbled into the restaurant, nearly fallen twice, she's in rare form. She likes this place for its plaid and floral decor, its country clutter, for the open-aired room with its "genuine" fireplace, though nothing is genuine about the glassed in Heatilater. It's lunch out, away from the Manor, but by now we are at the tail end of it. She is using her fork to push a piece of chocolate cheesecake around on her plate as though chasing it. My subtext: *Get it, Mom, get that piece of cake before it escapes.* I resist the temptation to reach over with my own fork, push the errant piece onto hers.

Her shirt is spackled with mayo from her leaky chicken wrap, and three napkins lay crumpled on the floor. But she wants this final smidgen of chocolate cheesecake and has announced to the locals at the next table that "it's really delicious." The next table snickers. The man shakes his head and I wonder when I should break down and smack him. Then it occurs to me that she's been pushing that cake away as much as she has been trying to spear it. To delay her return to the Manor? Cheap trick, Mom, but unnecessary; the cheesecake has developed its own defense, rolling around the plate like a miniature cat. After what seems like two weeks, she puts her fork down and looks at the group seated at a long table nearby. The place is crowded.

"Everybody comes here." Today, her speech is clear. Today, she insisted on her cane instead of the free-to-go-out wheelchair the Manor provides for off-campus visits. She hates the deference people offer when she uses the wheelchair. She can't hear well in groups anymore, can't see small print, can't figure out the TV remote, and most of all she is incontinent. But she notices that everyone comes here and she is a part of it. In recent weeks, she's come to accept public help from Marijo and me only because otherwise she rarely gets out of the Manor, thus today's cheesecake. Lately, when we are in public with her, she drops her sharpness and announces, "This is my daughter. Isn't she wonderful?" At first, I was convinced she said this to fling the cleaver of guilt right to my heart, but when I look at her face, I see it's just her butter-knife face—no cleaver: just spreading it on thick.

She gives the cake another forky push. Another push to the lip of the plate. The chocolate piece teeters and escapes, leaps from plate to table, doing a little back flip to show off the raspberry icing. It rests for a second, planning its next move.

"Oh shit," she says. Her filter is shifting too. The portly man at the next table snickers. Now she's pushing the piece around the table, her fork hand trembling.

I lean over the plate, and of the remaining larger chunk—which we were sharing—I fork a half, lift my own fork, and chew with concentration worthy of a dog worrying a bone. I will not yell at her to *leave the damned cake alone, to stop playing with her food* (gosh, in her own words even). I chew slowly, watching her chase the cake to the edge of the table, her fork hovering with helicopter strategy.

She goes after the piece, pushing the fork over the plastic cloth like a shovel, leaving a smear of raspberry. The people nearby hide smiles under tidy napkins. I see her chin lift in that *don't you look at me* defiance. Suddenly I want to defend her. I have never defended her, only defended myself from her. I want to shout, *We'll all be here someday.*

The impulse is new in me. We are here, two women with forks, one is trying to kill something that seems alive, the other is trying not to kill anything—but she's thinking about it. Once I use my own fork to push her piece back toward her, and she says, lickety-split, "I can do it." And whaps my wrist with her fork. The man next to us spits into his coffee. Nothing about this is quiet.

God help me.

Then she looks up, studies my shoulder-cut blouse, says pointedly, "So, is that what they're wearing now? Holes in the shoulder?"

I need this like I need a hole in the head.

We are being mean to each other. Because of this living, breathing cake of history. I don't know what I am doing here, trying to create camaraderie out of mustard and soiled napkins. I stare at the raspberry smear as if I could read it, and it happens again, the bright pink of memory rises: the bright pink cake of my childhood, the Barbie-doll birthday cakes, angel food baked with a hole in the middle for the doll to slip into, then you "dress" the doll with ruffles of icing frothed into pink rows up and down the cake, right up over her bodice. The cake was the gown, and that's what you ate. Mom spent hours on those Barbie-doll cakes, ornamenting them with frosted roses and garlands of sweet. We were supposed to cut the pieces from the back first, to let everyone see the masterpiece of loveliness for as long as possible, that model of princessy femininity. Then she'd caution—*not too big a piece for you girls.* The message: look like this but don't enjoy the taste. Once when she had presented a doll cake to me, a birthday in my teens, I put my whole face into it, ruining the beauty. I meant it as a joke, smearing my face with all that sugary froth that I wasn't supposed to eat, not really—defying her mixed message of gift and self-discipline. She never made me another one.

My coffee's gone cold, and I am no longer hungry. The laughter at the next table is no joke. I hand her another napkin, she dabs her mouth, misses the mustard, and the fourth napkin drops to the floor. The cake piece? Still tabled.

She stares at it. "You want it?" she asks.

"No thanks." What I had forgotten: she had spent hours on a cake that I ruined.

Her hands go still on her lap. Fork abandoned. The air cools. The restaurant quiets. She wants her sweets, she wants her dessert, she wants to be able to lift her food on her own. She wants no help from me. She wants to eat out. She wants to be with people. Now her hands rest like quiet birds on her lap, smeared with crumbs of a silent cake we cannot speak to each other.

We are at a cake stalemate. Someone needs to make a move. I lift my fork, stab the battered chocolate, and then carefully turn the fork and hand it to her. She looks at me steadily, and I wait—will she take the cake, battered as it is? She lifts her hand, grasps, gets the fork to her mouth, and beat up as it is, she chews slowly, savoring it. She looks at me and I think she's going to tell me how good it was, but instead she announces, "Not alive anymore." Cheesecake, dead. This is where we are now. I miss that she accepted the fork.

TEA LEAVES I

> Tasseography (also known as tasseomancy) is the art of
> identifying symbols and interpreting messages found
> in the shapes and configurations of tea leaves.
>
> —Aliza Kelly Faragher, "Your Essential Guide to Tasseography,
> the Practice of Reading Tea Leaves," *Allure*, May 7, 2018, https://www
> .allure.com/story/how-to-read-tea-leaves-tasseography

At last I find I must look at her past, direct some energy there, see if I can understand what happened in her childhood that then happened to us. Truth is, she's been as forthcoming as a bank vault reinforced against the apocalypse. Her privacy is as hard-shelled as her temper is deflective. She'd be so pissed that I'm writing this.

Why on earth?

Mom, it's how I might come to see it all differently.

Just see what it gets you.

She almost spits. So, I turn to memory, faulty as it is. And yes, hearsay. The first thing that comes to mind is *tea leaf*.

Mom had the hoarding tendencies of Depression-era survivors and rarely threw away anything that had an iota of life left in it. *Keep it for backup.* She loved "old things" in general, but she collected one thing with dedication, a pattern of ironstone china called Tea Leaf. That collection, which is not china at all but its bastard cousin, ironstone, contains some of her origin stories. Perhaps here, pieces of her that I can recognize and build from. A way to know her.

> It may sound obvious, but in order to read tea
> leaves, you must first brew a cup of tea.
>
> —Faragher, "Your Essential Guide to Tasseography"

Only at Christmas does my mother reach up, lift the sacred dish carefully down, dust it, and pile it with wild-gathered black walnuts, finally dried enough for cracking. The walnuts, pyramided like balls of hard dirt in the compote dish, stack a rough irony against the winter-white gleam of the ironstone china, the elegant curve of the pedestal, the coppery scallop on the edges.

During the year, the pedestal compote sits pretentiously on the top shelf of cheap oak-veneer entertainment center in Mom and Dad's river house. The dish, graceful, Greek style, is one of five pieces saved from the fires, all in that rare tea-leaf pattern.

She places a smaller white dish next to the compote, and while my father watches Huntley and Brinkley, he lifts one walnut at a time from the compote dish, cracks it, pries out the meat, and fingers the nuts into a plastic Tupperware on his lap, eating as many as he drops into the container. He drops the broken shells into the small bowl. Those black walnuts that survive his ferocious snacking she will mix into batter for sweet bread and give to family at Christmas. When the compote dish is empty, she will wipe out the shards, its coppery three-leafed pattern glowing in the palm of the empty bowl, and she will sit down and study the pattern as if seeking prophesy, as if the empty interior served as oracle.

> When prompted with a question, the leaves reveal hidden blockages,
> offer advice, and even forecast the future. These mystical messages are
> embedded within the wet leaves' shape, density, color, and placement.
>
> —Faragher, "Your Essential Guide to Tasseography"

Like yeast for sourdough, these starter pieces were handed down to Mom, from the 1800s, and she added to them over the decades, always trying for a set of twelve. Over the years, as I watched her, I found myself more fascinated by her fascination than with the objects themselves. That elegant simplicity, the three-leafed tea pattern kept her attention. If I lift one, read the tea leaf at the bottom, tragedy comes down first from my mother's mother, Julia Cox. My grandmother.

From their Belgian and Flemish roots, the Coxes settled in Michigan in the early 1880s. Julia was born at the latter end of the decade, in the spring of 1888. They had some success, a little affluence to the degree that when Julia was a child, a dressmaker would come to the farmhouse to measure her for dresses. The tea leaf pieces belonged to Julia's mother, Octavia Correyn Cox (my great-grandmother), and would have been housed somewhere in that Weare Township home. Julia and her mother would have held them, perhaps studied them too.

I remember Julia as a short, plump, warm-hearted woman who loved to crochet, tat, wear vivid hats with peacock feathers, and yes, laugh. I didn't know her well, but I have the sense that Julia was raised with some protection and even some comforts, a few pretty things, thus the tea leaf, until her own mother became ill with cancer, and Julia was thrust into caring for a mother who died in their home when Julia was just sixteen. She was the only woman on that farm.

But one of the men, a hired hand, is also in this history. Joseph Van Agtmael, my mother's father, was born in 1893 and immigrated from Essen, Belgium, entering the United States at Ellis Island at the age of fifteen. The family lore is that he was the eleventh child of his family, that his mother died shortly after his birth, that he was wet-nursed by his elder sister. If even half of that is true, it would be enough burden to carry into life. But there was no land for such a late-born son, little money, and few resources in Belgium. His brother Peter had immigrated before him, and Joseph followed suit in March 1909, crossing the Atlantic on the *Kroonland*, Red Star Line, third class. I believe he was alone.

Records at Ellis Island say "laborer."

He didn't speak English and was denigrated as a "greenhorn."

He made his way to Michigan to work off his passage, first for his brother Peter, and then for a local veterinarian, and finally for Cornelius Cox (who was from Flanders) at the farm in Weare Township in western Michigan, where he met that young Julia Cox, the boss's only daughter, that woman with her thick hair and a ready laugh. Somewhere in that second decade of the twentieth century, Joseph and Julia became more to each other than a boss's daughter and hired hand. I don't know if their intentions were made known to anyone before World War I broke out, but when the United States joined the war, Joseph, whom my mother once described as an "army man," enlisted and returned to Europe and fought in the countries near his homeland. The battle names handed down, Marne and Argonne, reveal that he probably saw the worst the Great War had to offer, but I've never been able to confirm his experience there. Family stories say that even though Joseph was not literate, he dictated letters to people who could write, and a correspondence with Julia evolved while he was overseas.

What I know for sure is that after that war, he came home to Oceana County, to the Coxes, and made his intentions clear. Joseph and Julia were married one year to the day after Armistice Day, on the first anniversary of peace-making, in 1919, a gesture that may have reflected his survival as much as their resilience. I remember him as slim, wiry, with clear blue eyes, a gaunt face, and a forever cigarette. Because of his experience with the vet, he was good with horses and large animals, but there was more. My mother once told Marijo that he was a horse whisperer, that he had that rare gift, and that people who couldn't afford vets would bring sick horses to him, and sometimes he could help in ways others could not. He planned to farm, but he also kept that deep connection with the horses. He took on and trained those big work horses, his own and others, to know the fields, follow the plows, attend the commands of farmers who needed their muscle. He did not yet feel the threat of the "iron horse" in the future. He had, by all accounts, a chance to make good.

I suspect Julia took with her the tea leaf pieces when she and Joseph settled on their own farm on section 23, Elbridge Township, fifteen miles straight east of Hart, an hour's buggy ride and a parish away from Weare, where the Coxes had lived and Julia had grown up. The Elbridge property was known for good soil, and my mother remembers the clearing process of cutting trees and burning fields.

There was a two-story farmhouse with a front porch. A big new barn. There were four children. Three survived. Mom, then Neil, and Robert. And that lost one? Rex. I know nothing about that boy, a brother to my mother, a baby who lived only a few days, but whose death sent Grandma Julia into depression and forced my mother into a caregiving role, like her mother before her, and that exposed her to both shame about her mother's debilitated state and her first aching sorrow.

I believe Mom felt her baby brother's loss deeply, perhaps because it estranged her from her own mother, and perhaps she needed to grieve herself, but her responsibilities kept her from that indulgence. If pressed, Mom would acknowledge this loss sharply, impatiently, "Yes, he died and of course it was terrible," then would close her mouth with a snap, her jaw thrust out, her silence final. Here are shadows that if she could not touch, she wouldn't let anyone else touch.

Grandma Julia was a tender soul, an uninspired cook, a resigned wife, a skilled needleworker who could tackle the most difficult patterns with ease, but she was not a terribly complicated or sophisticated person. She was, by all accounts, gentle and kind. I realize now she must have been an inexperienced mother who didn't quite have it in her to push or to lead her children. Or know how to manage Joseph's boomeranging moods. By the time Mom was a sophomore in high school, poverty seems to have overtaken them. On school mornings, Mom walked over a mile south to a tiny grocery store, where she caught a ride that then took her to a place where a bus would pick her up. But with the unpredictable weather, lack of proper footwear, inconsistency with that ride, the challenges were too great, and she did what many in her generation did. She quit high school in her junior year to work on the farm. Contributing to that decision may have been the social stigma: her father had garnered a reputation as a drinker. She admitted once that though he could be fun, especially playing cards, if he was in his cups, he turned mean. Then she'd say, "But never speak ill of the dead." She'd refuse to say more.

I believe that Julia loved Joe deeply but wouldn't stand up to him, and when his drinking was out of control, it would be her own daughter to whom she turned. Julia depended on my mother. I also suspect she didn't know how to be a mother to her daughter, Ruth, who was perceptive and sensitive to a fault and already saw things that others didn't. What I have come to believe: my mother grew up tender, without much maternal nurturing, with expectations that may have been beyond her ken, and with a father's broken drive and bitter addiction nipping at her heels. Still, this doesn't unlock my mother's heart to me.

> The person seeking answers in the divination practice—
> whether it be you or someone else—is referred to as
> the querent. Specificity is very important here, so be
> sure to formulate a clear and concise question.
>
> —Faragher, "Your Essential Guide to Tasseography"

Mine are not questions with specificity, let alone concision. Mine are why questions.

Here's one thing. An odd thing. My mother had childhood acne that lingered into her adulthood, probably caused by poor diet and hygiene. She told me that Grandma Julia's menu for evening meals was fried pork or bacon, fried potatoes in the pork grease, and maybe a vegetable cooked to mush, also fried in animal fat. The family bathed once a week, for church on Sunday, and as to their daily ablutions, I'm not sure how much hot water was involved. None of that addresses my mother's unaddressed stress: her own mother's depression, her father's drink and his tongue, brutal Depression-era frugality. She once reported that at school she had been called "pock head." Her self-consciousness about her skin was a concern she spoke of often.

Then, at seventeen, a year or so after she quit school, she left the farm. I don't know the details, but the word *escape* comes to mind. I think it was like that: she escaped that struggling rural Elbridge farm. She went to, of all places, Chicago.

Two stories survive that time: Through—and this I did not expect—my father's older sister, Catherine Oomen, a church friend who had found work in Chicago, my mother made contacts to be hired as a housekeeper. When my mom left her parents' farm, she took the long train south along the coast of Lake Michigan to meet a man who she would know by a carnation in his lapel. He met her at the Adams station in Chicago.

In a moment of weakness, she told me that when they met on that train platform, he was cold to her and barely took her in. He didn't like her looks. He didn't like her skin. He thought she had an infection. He didn't like her. After a few days as a cleaning maid, she was "let go," layering shame on shame. That acne. That legacy of the greenhorn. I try to imagine this moment for her, how she would become obsessed with looking right, overly concerned with impressions, and by proxy, with what her surrogates—her children—also would look like.

As a mother, she worried about her children's skin inordinately and feared for us the scarring she carried—though by the time I really looked at her skin, the damage had healed, and there were few traces. She made up for this self-perceived flaw with a heightened consciousness: not only how she dressed, or if she had proper clothes for an occasion, but if her kids were *presentable*. As if we would meet royalty. Limited as our circumstances were, she sewed or altered all our clothing, cleverly disguising high-end hand-me-downs and remnants, creatively insisting on us looking of better class than we were. Except for when we were doing field work—then she wanted us in our oldest clothes.

But that job in Chicago, the one from which she was fired, is not the end of the story.

Somehow, despite the acne, she found another job, as "a governess" (her word, though the duties she described were a nanny's) in a fine mansion owned by the Brown family in Lake Forest. This time, the rapport was right, and she worked for the Browns for nearly two years, caring for the Browns' children. There she also learned the trappings of class: how to set a correct table, mangle linens, fold napkins, use a soup spoon and little fork, how to cut and display fresh flowers, and even proper manners. She learned to pour coffee with grace, and yes, to lift a cup and sip tea properly, without slurping. She learned what formality looked like, what money and proper behavior really did to make appearances convincing. And as I look at her tea leaf, I wonder if this small success with the Browns, this insight into another world, may have also given her a small sense of superiority.

She also discovered friends and a social life. She attended dances with other young women, refugees from rural poverty, and with them, drove in old Model Ts to Geneva, outside of Chicago, where they would attend Grange dances, and meet boys, mostly soldiers preparing for what would become World War II. Here, it seems, almost a stability, a pattern of confident youth.

> How the symbols interact with other, nearby symbols
> can change their meanings, as well. For example, hands
> are interpreted in relation to what's near them, such as
> what they are pointing toward or reaching toward.
>
> —Lindsey Goodwin, "Tasseography Symbols for Reading Coffee or Tea
> Leaves," *Spruce Eats*, May 29, 2021, https://www.thespruceeats.com
> /tasseography-tea-leaf-reading-symbols-765838

The tea leaves could call her back. The call came in 1940. An accident. Hands point back to the farm, to Elbridge Township to nurse her injured father, Joseph, after a car crash so serious the caretaking was beyond her mother Julia's capacity. His back broken, jaw shattered, maybe a head injury. *Come home.* Mom said only that it was very hard to leave the two children she had cared for. Joseph lived through his injuries, but he didn't stop drinking. After he recovered, World War II commenced. Mom's family listened to the news about the Japanese bombing Pearl Harbor on a radio the size of a china hutch in the shabby living room of Joseph and Julia's home, and Mom said only, "We knew it would be bad."

Her brother Robert promptly enlisted and was sent to Guam.

Shortly, a call for nurses went out to the rural communities. So many nurses had signed on to WAC that there was a shortage at home. Mom picked orchard fruit, cherries and peaches, and worked in fields all that summer to earn enough money to enter nurses training. She lied on her application, claiming she had graduated high school—and she taught herself enough of the required algebra to pass the entry tests for nurses training. Tenacity, the good side of stubbornness, was on her side, as was that dogged need (or drive) to make something of herself.

What she had learned in Chicago was that there was more to life, and that it just might be possible to have some of it. Being a nurse might be the beginning. And by then, based on photographs, her skin had cleared. Her fine Belgian bones and thick hair glow. In photos taken during those years of nurses training, she looks happier than in any other photos of her entire life.

In nursing, she discovered an identity and satisfaction in practical knowing: break a fever, set a bone, clean a wound, heal a cut. Her hands comforted the sick—she felt at home in this work and thrived. Again, a social life. In that time, soldiers everywhere, waiting to ship out. She met someone, a soldier. From the Plains states, Kansas or Nebraska. They became engaged. She wrote steadily to him, and he to her, while he was overseas and she was training under the nuns at the Manistee Hospital. He was killed in action in the second year of the war. There is a story that she received the telegram while she was working on one of the wards at the hospital. She told the charge nurse, a nun. The Sister said the only way to survive was through work. My mother worked three shifts until she collapsed.

She destroyed the letters.

That loss, that difficult and incredible loss, gives me a picture of someone I almost understand.

> Also, the overall placement of symbols in the cup
> can change their meanings. Some readers divide the
> cup into sections to read with regard to the wish or
> question the reader has focused on for the reading.
> —Goodwin, "Tasseography Symbols for Reading Coffee or Tea Leaves"

Then, from other old letters written by her best friend, I learn a complication. She had sent back his ring before he was killed. She had backed out of the engagement. Suddenly, a whole different light falls on that relationship. She had already broken with him? Would she have wondered if he had received the letter, if he had the ring with him when he died, if he had gone into battle with her in his mind? Would her skin have been clear, but her conscience riddled with the acne of guilt? Would this experience create the obsessive caution I felt in her about her own emotions? Or just plain and pervasive regret?

The leaves turn yet again.

Still, she was capable and quick, organized and efficient, and from what I've gleaned, doctors liked to work with her because she could anticipate what they needed, and she didn't question them. She was offered a position as a nurse office manager in Hart with a doctor she liked. She refused, saying publicly that she preferred being closer to the patients. This may have been true, but once again, in a moment of rare camaraderie, she admitted that her father, Joseph, had become a serious threat, that he would come to the doctor's office to publicly beg for money so he could drink. She said, "He would make a scene. I couldn't risk that."

From these dark shards, I imagine the scene: Joseph staggers into a country doctor's office, bumbling through the waiting room, coming to the desk, begging for a few dollars, shouting when she refuses. I see her embarrassment, his wheedling. A doctor, hearing the ruckus, enters the waiting area, sends Joseph away sternly or leads him out, perhaps tosses him, staggering, onto the streets. I see the patients in a small-town office watching, not always with sympathy. That sniff. Those dirt farmers.

A leaf unfolds in the tea cup: had she thought the nursing profession would keep her safe, and had she become confident and proud, thus she couldn't bear the humiliation—a near phobia to her—when her father shamed her? Even as a child, I understood shame was a living beast growling at every turn in our house. Does it go back to being a *pock head*? Her father being a greenhorn? Did the acne of her childhood simply turn into the shame of any public blemish brought on by her father's drunkenness? Those things may contribute but I suspect it's deeper.

After the war, my mother, Ruth Jean Van Agtmael, married John Cornelius Oomen, a childhood friend, my too quiet father. He and Mom had known each other as children, and their families were church friends, but though quick and smart, he was too reserved for the woman she was becoming. In World War II, he had served two military tours in Africa and Italy, served under General Patton, and may have had an Italian girlfriend. When he returned, late in 1945, she didn't like him, thought he was "stuck-up, even quieter than he had been before the war. Later, again in a camaraderie it has been hard to reclaim, she told me he had forgotten how to be with women.

So much for the Italian girlfriend.

Here, another leaf, crumpled but floated many times, a story that when John and Ruth were barely into their teens, long before the war, their families had attended the county fair together. As they walked the fairway, he had said to her, "Aw, let's get married." And she had said, "Well sure." It was, they always said, just a joke. But they both remembered it. Repeated it. A decade and a world war later, in July 1947, she bought an inexpensive dress of white ruffled organza, the design influenced by the movie *Gone with the Wind*. She cooked the church lunch for forty on her own the morning before she married. She did it to make everything as nice, as classy, as she could, but also to keep it as cheap as she could, a pattern that stuck a lifetime and annoyed me no end.

She was twenty-seven when she married. She gave up nursing, and after three childless years, she took iodine to treat a deficiency, promptly got pregnant, and we five arrived, all within six and a half years. It goes without saying, is almost cliché, that we were hard, the farm was hard, the living was hard. She worked constantly and with an intensity I feel in my own bones that broke her spirit and bent her back, literally, with slipped disks and the eventual spinal stenosis that makes an invalid of her now. Under domestic pressure, physically and mentally exhausted, she spiraled in and out of her growing nervous terrors, which she did not suffer in silence.

I was firstborn and saw it evolve but could not divine the source.

It should be observed that some cups when examined will
present no features of interest, or will be so clouded and
muddled that no clear meaning is to be read in them. . . . Either
the consultant has not concentrated his or her attention upon
the business in hand when turning the cup, or his destiny is
so obscured by the indecision of his mind or the vagueness
of his ideas that it is unable to manifest itself by symbols.

—a Highland seer, "Tea-Cup Reading and Fortune Telling by Tea
Leaves," Electric Scotland, https://www.electricscotland.com/history
/articles/tealeaves.htm

She was hospitalized three times that I remember: bouts of breathlessness, chest pain, and sometimes hysteria, a lashing out that
sent us scattering. Sometimes doctors said it was for her bad back,
that bad disk, sometimes they said, "nerves" or "exhaustion," fudg-
ing the truth. They only kept her, or perhaps she would only stay,
for a few days, a week at most. Then she came home, sometimes
rested briefly, but soon, always too soon, she was working again
with a concentration and self-imposed discipline that was nearly
inhuman. There would be periods (usually only days) of calm, a pattern that felt "normal," a routine both welcomed and fragile, during
which she would mother and teach and offer up her quick dry wit,
where her charm would reign and there would be some laughter,
but then the mood would turn, quick as wax hardening, toward
something opaque and brittle. Publicly, she was always poised. It
was uncanny—how gracious she could be to people in our community, our church. Privately, she was unpredictable. Sometimes lov-
ing but we never knew what would cause the shift, never understood when we would face the onslaught. And we, her children,
were strong-willed—did I say that? I don't doubt we tried every
nerve in her body. I don't doubt we were a pain in the ass.

Decades after I'd left her and was working with high school children who had anxiety disorders, a trauma-broken teenaged girl
said, with such clear self-perception that it was like she shot an
electric arrow into my consciousness, "When I'm anxious I can't
help lashing out . . . I just feel the anger gush and explode out of
me." The metaphor leapt, "lashing out, gush and explode," and a

thought arrived like that lightning. Did Mom have an undiagnosed anxiety disorder, or some kind of PTSD? How could I have missed this? Then too, later, my sisters and I would learn about adult children of alcoholics—that damage. Even so, the one time I suggested to Mom that she might want to see a specialist about her moods, her *nerves*—as she called them—she went ballistic. I walked out. By then, too much ornery between us. I could not know.

What she knew that we didn't, the tea leaf of her childhood, the tea of secrecy, the ironstone of silence and the firing of anxiety, stayed with her and her alone.

THE CUP

Natalie, one of the residents at the Manor, along with six other residents plus my mother and me, crowd around an eight-top dining room table like planets, staring at the circular tray in the center. Natalie asks, not for the first time, "What way is east?"

Susan, the director of activities, points to the window.

Natalie sniffs. "I must be turned around." She looks out the east window, mutters, "Oh hell."

I'm here because Mom has, if it were possible, withdrawn further into hiding than ever before. The aides have reported her sitting in the dark of her room and refusing to interact. They've said, "Ruth's *reclusive*," a word analogous with hermits and cave dwellers. When I asked Mom about how she felt, she'd snapped, "I'm bored." When I pressed her to make friends with a neighbor lady recently moved into the room next to her, she said, "She's Lutheran." Mom's placed Lutherans in the same category as the Methodists.

Marijo and I are worried sick. We had assumed she'd settle in over time, that she'd enjoy the social aspects, make friends, that the ease of responsibility would help her relax and she'd find some activity to enjoy. Manor life is not going according to plan. Even with bingo, Sittercise, and singalongs, she's not participating. So, I'm sitting in, researching activities to learn what or who might capture her attention, she who, when the mood once struck her, could be a first-rate social butterfly. Our plan: find out what the problem is, solve it. That simple.

Today she's wearing her snooty look.

Natalie takes a breath.

"East," Susan points to the window.

Mom sighs.

On the table, Styrofoam cups, a bag of dirt, an envelope of seeds. One envelope. A dozen or so seeds. They are planting sunflowers, one seed a piece.

You're kidding, right?

Susan gives directions. First, pass around the cups. Once in hand, stare into it for a while, this plain Styrofoam cup. It must be studied, the curved white emptiness. Write your name on the rim. For some, names never arrive. In that case, Susan is keeper of the names: if a name is lost, she will find it for you. And help write it. Some folks know their names, but not what the white cup is, and the what-to-do-about-it is often pure guesswork. Some can't remember the way their hands should work, some forget how letters work. For some, no problem; they help the others. Mom knows her name, writes it despite the uncertain surface. The name-on-your-cup identification takes about ten minutes. Mom is silent and staring. This can only get worse.

Next. Dirt in the cup. Susan pours a big bag of homogenized compost into a bowl and passes it like Sunday dinner. I help Mom spoon potting soil. She spills but says nothing. I wipe the table with the dorsal side of my hand, and she humphs.

Susan walks around, placing seeds next to the cup as though they were pencils for a test.

One fucking seed. For a woman whose garden was once a sprawling of acres, hundreds of thriving seedlings, six long bean rows, twelve of corn. That single sunflower? An insult. Mom never even grew sunflowers because "birds just get 'em." As an adult, I defiantly grew sunflowers. Let the birds at them. That was how we rolled.

Natalie is at it again. "What way is . . . ?"

East. The heads of the sunflowers always faced the morning. They knew east.

Susan carries on. "After you've filled the cup, stick your index finger in the dirt, press down to make a hole, an indentation that will leave a little space around the seed." Susan opens the package, circles the room. "I've placed a seed in front of you."

"Is that a bug?"

"You can pick it up."

"It's a bug."

"It's a big seed."

Still, the sunflower seed is hard to see if your eyeglass prescription has not been changed for ten years because your Medicare won't cover it. Mom picks the seed up slowly, examining it suspiciously. *Please God, let her know.* She does.

From Susan's control center, "Drop the seed into the hole." Tricky because there is no sure way to keep the hand from wavering wild as a moth's flight. But Mom gets it the first time. A couple of folks pop the seeds in their mouths. Susan commands, "Spit those out." There is a lot of saliva in the air for a moment. Susan checks that each seed is properly placed. Susan demonstrates how to cover the seeds. Everyone at the table seems able, pressing the dirt, slipping fingers into the interior. Press press press. Now, set the cup back in the tray. Eight cups filled with soil and one seed each.

Natalie wants to know. "Should we water the plants?"

That's when Susan explains the contest. "The plants will be watered for the residents, all the same amount."

"Why can't we water them?"

"You residents tend to overwater them," she smiles.

"How do you know?" Carl asks pointedly.

"They turn yellow and die." Message: *Don't mess with watering. Or Susan.* "You can observe the sprouts and mark the days until the seedlings can be transplanted outside.

So, planting sunflowers is an exercise designed for those who may have lost time. Susan's offering an activity that memory-compromised residents might grasp, that they can watch and measure, the size of seedling against the days of ... general boredom.

Mom sighs. Of course she does. Her garden times stand bright and clear. She knew the way a garden became a companion, like another child, plants changing daily, the growth erratic and fragile, then steady as a healthy child. How many gardens had she planted? Forty? Fifty?

"What do we win?" Carl again. Something must always be won.

Susan says, "Oh, we give prizes for the tallest, biggest around, shortest, smallest, even the one with most seeds."

"Whose gonna count those?" He's having none of it.

At this point, I catch a bit of his smart-ass and ask about fertilizing the seeds, and glancing sideways, wink at Mom. Unbelievably she winks back. Slip a little 12-12-12 in the cup.

Susan's way ahead, "We know that fertilizer trick." *Fertilizer trick?* She announces that the staff will fertilize all the sunflowers just the same, same time, same amount, so it's just the plant that makes the difference, except maybe, here she smiles, *if you talk to it.* "That's what you can do to encourage growth."

My mother stares hard. She knows: this woman is certifiable.

Because of course Mom remembers tomatoes spilling over their stakes, sweet corn so tall that to walk the rows was to enter green and golden canyons—the sweet corn that at least half the time raccoons stripped before we did. The garden was practical, provided for a family. You planted, watered, and yes, considered the proportions of fertilizer, the schedule of application. Talk to a plant? Lordy.

Susan isn't letting up, "Last year some family member didn't know that the staff fertilized the seedlings, so played smarty-pants and fertilized the resident's seedlings on the sneak. The sunflower died." A few residents shake their heads.

No cheating on the sunflowers.

Susan collects the seeded cups and lines them up on the tray, tiny dark ponds in the center of the table. Everyone stares. In the silence, Natalie keeps turning this way and that, and sometimes Susan touches her arm to get her to stop. Then they settle, study the cup with a deep and perfect concentration. *Yeah Mom, I get it. We're done here.* I stand, look down, and my mother sends me her stink eye. I sink again. We are, apparently, not bored enough.

Then it happens. From the kitchen counter, Susan turns with another tray in her hands, asks, "Who wants hot chocolate?" The compass stops, points. Sudden shift, eyes up, faces turn in unison. They knew this was coming? The old sugar of hot chocolate? Of course.

My mother gives me her other look, her get-your-ass-off-the-chair-and-help look. I stand, help Susan tear the packages and pour in the hot water. We stir the powder and carry the mugs. This time the old hands reach with little hesitation; they wrap their fingers around the warmth with affection, nearly tenderness.

Natalie looks up at me, "It's that way, isn't it?" And she points to the window.

I say, "There you go, you remember."

She looks hurt. *Oh, shoot.* She does not remember the way I do, but the idea of remembering and not remembering is one concept she does half remember, that she half knows she does not have anymore. I feel like shit. For her, for all of them. Memory is how things are changing, in these small unmomentous shards, a loss almost measurable.

But then, just like that, she asks again, "What way's east?"

Even Susan of eternal patience has had enough, snaps, "The way the sun comes up."

"Well, why didn't you say that." And Natalie smiles a huge smile as if that answers all the great questions. Such is redemption here at the Manor.

Then, "But where does it go down?"

"West," my mother answers clearly. She nods into her cup with the kind of vehemence I have not seen for weeks. West. Mom's hands in the dirt, in the garden, always in the *eastern* light. Squash, melons, oh the muskmelons, always small—too far north for big ones—but still tasty, wrinkled as brains, resting in the dirt, sweet and half buried, vines dying like snakes around them, waiting for her hands to lift and break them. Morning work, always. The constant garden in the morning. But now, this is western light. Western light drives my mother to her room, away from interactions that would keep life interesting. End-of-day light. West is her current direction, the one she lives now. I want east for her.

Susan clears the seed cups, placing them in a long tray for the windowsill or wherever they will go to be spoken to. Moves on to the hot chocolate cups.

Mom plucks her sleeve, wadding her Kleenex, and finally says, "Let's go."

Leaving the room, we hear Natalie ask again. Mom's opinionated voice rises as she crosses the threshold of the door, "Well, she's lost it." I choke down a whoop of laughter, elbowing her into 116 before she can deliver any more grande dame quips.

She looks around her room, searching. Out of the blue, "Where is that cup?"

"What cup?"

"The cup with the dirt."

"They're going to set them all together in the sun room."

Her voice is tearful. "Wasn't I supposed to watch it?" Querulous, nearly panicked. "I was supposed to take care of something." Her eyes fill, "Wasn't I?" And just as suddenly, she's angry. "Don't they know I've got too much work to do. What am I supposed to do now?"

Suddenly she's not quite in this moment. She's home on the farm, pressured and too busy, with nothing extra to give to whatever was in that cup. She remembers only responsibility, that there was something she was meant to do. She doesn't remember the seed. She doesn't remember that single seed, only the pressure. My voice from a distant place, "They kept the cup, Mom. Susan and the aides. They'll keep it safe, take care of it for you."

She looks at me as though I have told her a lie, then decides to believe. Her relief is a tangible breath filling the air between us. "I don't have to worry about it then."

She forgot the seed, forgot the tiny shard of garden she was given. An answer rockets into the too quiet room. She's not being reclusive, not looking for purpose or interaction. She's forgetting. That's what she's doing. And if she is forgetting the single seed that would have been the link to all the gardens of her life, how long do we have, she and I, to relearn the cardinal directions?

MCDONALD'S AT
THE MANOR

She leans, lifts, and slides; leans, lifts, and slides. We learn her physical status via the hallway, the longest corridor of the Manor, from an aluminum walker, not a wheelchair. That's how residents get exercise. Walk the long hall. Lean, lift, and slide. Push forward.

She looks up, "I'm just here for the winter. That's why." If she can take the long walk down the long hall every day, she will go home in the spring. We nod. It's her third winter.

The once-relied upon cane—*Damn thing catches on the rugs*—has been retired. But the walker is slow; the lean, lift, slide, the four-legged weight shift makes her impatient even as it stabilizes. She steadies her balance, positions her hands, and rolls forward, clomping, its "feet" shoed in yellow tennis balls. Every time, she looks up daunted, says, "What a long hallway." Her breaths are raspy, ghosts of her once swift and pounding steps across her kitchen, her yards, gardens, fields, her rush everywhere. *Rush* was a word she believed in and embodied. For her, *rush* was a fruitful word. Now, *push*. Lean, lift, and slide.

Maybe a hundred feet, twelve rooms lined up on each side.

Slowly pass the laundry closet. Slowly pass Evelyn and Margo's rooms; mention that they live with two other women in a ward of four. Wave to Evelyn and Margo. Make for the nurses' station; stop to chat, slow the ragged breathing. Slowly, pass the room where the bedridden woman exists in a fetal position (stroke?) while her husband watches reruns of *Gunsmoke*. The room hurts her eyes. Look away. Pass another ward. Rest again, peer in, announce, "That's the men's ward," in a disgusted tone—"They smell funny, don't they?" Pass the library—"Such a pretty room"—a tiny chapel—"I don't know why they use it for storage"—and finally into the community room, that spacious but deceptive place that pretends its name. It's usually empty, a cul de-sac of sorts. More plainly, a dead end. She turns around her walker, settles heavily into a chair. This room, bloated with overstuffed flowered couches and those fancy lamps replicating some long-gone European era, contains all the grace of worn-out melancholy. Even though the broad windows banking the south view are ornamented with flouncy mauve curtains, everything sags with a wilted cheer that hails the eighties. The place could use an overhaul.

I set up a card table, suddenly wishing I had a cloth—why don't I think of these things? Marijo would have; it's she who wisely suggested these indoor "picnics." Since Mom refuses a wheelchair, getting her out now means flirting with the disaster of a fall. So, we've taken to bringing in McDonald's to the Manor, thus avoiding the institutional food and the dead silence of the elders' lunch table all in one fell swoop. But after the long hall, the fries are dead cold.

I ladle salt on the fries anyway, unwrap and ketchup the burger, halve it. As she wolfs, she misses that I toss away my top bun and barely eat my smaller half. I like McDonald's about as much as I like sour milk. But she loves it, the first "easy" food of her life, meals that came quick and fully prepared, salty and cheap with some meat—a poor replica of her own onion-laden meatloaf patties from her own cast-iron pans.

I watch her eat, leaning toward her, parental in case she needs help. She hates that I sometimes "mother" her, I who never wanted to be a mother. This is hard, a thought that pushes sideways, but if I enter this question, an answer rises like a moon from fog. I am not a mother, in part because I saw that we did not make her happy. I remember her once, in the front yard, trying to sit for a minute under that great and calming tree. We saw her, alone, and we didn't know she could rest, that she might need to rest, and we careened around her, shouting and defying her silence, her tears, her exhaustion—

for we knew we should be paramount. We refused her need, and she responded with her own shrill will. She mothered us, yes. She loved us, her five unruly ones, but she did not love being a mother. Hers was a life of willing herself toward work and love, but her anger could not be repressed. Hers became a powerful model for how not to live.

Another better reason for not being a mother, this one about myself: I am utterly unsuited to the job. People who know me really well don't argue when I say that; they don't say, "Oh you'll feel differently when you have one of your own." People who know me well have suggested I would leave a child in some big box store and be miles down the road before it would occur to me, *Oh, I had someone with me.* They know I wouldn't do this on purpose, but due rather to a rich combination of being so easily distracted I would forget I had a child and having a thought process so insular that yes, I would forget I had a child.

But now. Is this attention to physicality how a mother feels? I want to say something meaningful, but my language has become procedural: safety, hygiene, pain level, comfort, and nourishment. A mother's worries? People speak of this role reversal in the aging process as though it were natural, but it irritates me, feels like a test I cannot pass. Because in this reversal is also my mother's frustration—she didn't like motherhood and that feeling was, in some subtle way, communicated to me. Now, she's victim of the same underlying messaging. I slowly eat the burger I hate, trying to figure out if there's a way to make it palatable.

In the stillness of the community room, light pours in. She notices the sewing machine in the corner, a Baby Lock. She points to it. "One of the ladies uses it," she says, still chewing.

You did too, Mom. One of your best accomplishments. You taught your girls to sew.

Baby Lock, a name to initiate re-remembering, a practice I'm trying out as a way to keep some things in place for her. For me. "Mom, do you remember the three satin skirts you sewed for Marijo and Patti and me, that Christmas plaid, for a dinner at the church hall, and you took a picture of us all standing in a row."

"Satin? No, not satin." Her lips ziplock. Too fancy for her to admit. But it was, from a remnant for sure, a piece she would have found in the sale bin and scrimped for. But she's shaking her head. So, we will not remember the three daughters standing together in plaid satin pieced at the hems, not remember her pride as people complimented her girls' outfits.

"Do you remember a yellow dotted swiss dress with scalloped edges you made for me to wear to a school Valentine's Day party. You said I should choose pink." What a fight that was.

"You always liked yellow." She once told me righteously that yellow didn't look good on me. She's right. No accounting for my taste. But she gave in.

"You stayed up half the night so it would be ready in the morning."

"I did?"

"You hung it in the archway between the dining and living rooms so it was the first thing I saw when I came downstairs." A sweet surprise in that uncertain house.

She frowns, searching. "I let you wear a yellow dress to a Valentine's party?"

Another cul-de-sac. I take a different tack.

"Do you remember the quilt you made for me when I married David, the king-size Drunkard's Path pattern?" The pattern that's a metaphor for my life, not a drunken path but a circuitous route, color coordinated quarter turns that eventually shape a complex tessellation.

"Oh, that thing."

I could crow. A memory we both have.

Then she shakes her head and her long-ago words return. *You want that pattern? On your bed?* If she knew my quilt pattern was also called Solomon's Puzzle, would she have liked it better? Solomon's Puzzle, because the pattern can reshape itself a half dozen ways, reforming, redirecting the eye, resolving its own puzzle, that quarter turn fitting in and out of itself. Metaphor for . . . us.

"What were the colors?" I ask, for her benefit.

"Too dark."

Deep green leaf pattern, dark magenta, black borders.

"How long did it take?"

"I don't know, but I was glad to get rid of it."

A year of her time, that's how long.

Childhood scenes rise. Last week, I woke from a dream memory, a time before the troubles between us, of her teaching me to hem a dress, that hem stitch that takes forever to master, the bringing together of two edges, one marked with pins, one not, and somehow, I must keep it straight. In dream terror, I found I couldn't do it, could not draw the needle through the fabric to stitch a straight hem for the dress. I woke trembling in the decades old echo of her scolding. But still the truth is, she taught me to hem, to stitch, to survive. I'm remembering the wrong things, the scold but not the drive.

I take a hard breath. I'm tired of the lift, lean, and slide of us. I did not intend to stumble into this, my denial of her time and skill. Hemming satin that she could not afford, up all night with a yellow dotted swiss, a year to piece a king-sized quilt. She had done things for me that brought her no joy that she doesn't even remember. As we sit in the poor light of the community room, some shift begins in its step-by-step, quarter-turn route.

She looks at the table, yellow mustard smeared, and commands sharply, "Need to clean up this mess." Another quarter turn, this one to the dark colors. Forgiveness flies up, a terrified bird.

EGGS

High summer at the Manor. We push Mom's walker to the gazebo in the back yard of the Manor, where surrounded by dozens of daylilies, she stares at the flowers but no longer attempts to name them. I watch her crawl inside herself; she naps in the middle of visits now, perhaps because I honestly can't find enough lively conversation to keep us going.

Of my childhood, my mother once confessed that I had so many imaginary friends, she worried about me. "I never knew who you were talking to, so much chatter, or what kind of person they were. Scared me, who your mind took up with." It did not make her happy, the imaginaries. She also once told me that I was a child of *why*, always asking why this and why that. "You just did it for attention. You didn't really want to know the answer." How did she know that? I'm a deeply curious person, but was I also that manipulative?

Suddenly she rouses. "What building is that?" She raises her arthritic finger and points to the tidy red brick walls of a medical care facility, the full-scale nursing home right next door to the Manor. She used to know. "That's the Oceana County Medical Care Facility."

She studies the place as though seeing it for the first time. I don't remind her it's where her own mother (my Grandma Julia) lived for the last years of her life. I don't say it's where she may have to go, depending on factors Marijo and I are just beginning to grasp. Mom's money drains away like water through a sieve, just as her abilities to care for herself slip with each passing month. We've been trying to assess how to keep her here where care is still "assisted." And from that, Marijo and I are also trying to manage every penny, then accurately predict her entire future: how long she stays here, how long before she'll need full care. Of course, it's ridiculous. The real question is: how long do I have to know her—though I can't help but wonder what the chances are of that. I didn't think it would matter.

But with each stumbling memory that rises, I'm discovering it matters, the kind of mother she was. She knows things about me I don't know about myself—beyond who my imaginary friends were, beyond my "whys." What I understand: if she forgets me, the conflict with her that has defined me also ceases, and I have no witness to define myself against. And if I don't understand myself, how do I understand her? Us? And other things? Like what kind of daughter I am.

The scent of hay drifts on the air. The scent of farm country. Her country.

The door of the Manor opens behind us, and two of the residents shuffle out like slow ducks and head toward the gazebo. We make room.

I know them from the sunflower planting weeks ago.

"You remember these ladies, Mom. Natalie and Marie."

Mom says, "Pleased to meet you." Never mind they've all been coresidents for nearly a year.

Natalie looks around, asks, "What day is it?"

"July 31," I say. Apparently, Natalie's switched tracks in the interim. Dates instead of directions.

"Oh, July already. Summer."

Marie says, "Egg season." She too had a farm.

Natalie, suddenly, "Rhode Island Reds and Wyandottes. The rest don't lay very good."

I mull the beautiful names, "We had . . . white ones."

My mother throws me a dirty look. "Leghorns." *Oh.*

Marie approves, "Good ones, don't go so broody. Not like those hybrids."

Natalie says, "You need a good rooster, that's all."

Well, at least this is conversation. "At my home in Empire, we can raise chickens but not roosters." I tell them that people wanted to ban chickens entirely.

All in, heat rising in their faces: *How come? Whatwhatwhat?* Natalie asks, "Why on earth?"

Which is how I end up explaining chicken regulations, trying to simplify the rigmarole of rooster behavior and village politics. "The roosters wouldn't follow the rules about crowing only in the morning, and they were crowing at all hours." Blank faces turn to me. I fill in, "In a village, that disturbed people."

Marie, animated, schools me instead. "Crowing at night just means a predator's out there. Those chicken people shoulda said that. You got to get up and shoot the fox." I shudder: local villagers wielding guns in the middle of the night.

Natalie asks, "What day is it."

"July 31st," I tell her, thinking the word *boring* so loudly it could be heard by them all.

"You can get an egg a day off every one of 'em in this light." Well, that then.

Marie nods, turns to me, asks "What kind you got?"

"I don't have chickens." I assumed this was clear.

"You buy eggs in the store?" They shake their heads.

"Too expensive," Marie says, tsking. Then she picks up as if nothing had interrupted her previous thought, "Not just fox. Dogs too get after 'em. You know, dogs go bad, break in. The roosters know. Hound slinking through the fence. Sets 'em right off. Roosters spur their noses and eyes, hightail 'em straight out. Protect those girls." By "girls" she means hens, I guess.

Natalie pitches in, "Sometimes other roosters too, and then other dogs go off too. All through the neighborhood. Some good, some bad, but all awake. Ruckus could wake the dead."

"How do you know which one's good and which bad?" I ask, thinking I have rarely been so weirdly absorbed in conversation, let alone about chickens.

"The good ones stay home."

Well yes, I think. A message from the past; stay home. I would not stay home, did not value the safety of the roost. Before I left for college even, the restless urge to escape ran my defiance. My learning to sew, Mom's deepest lesson, had ironically given me a way out. Trips with Mom's beloved 4-H club—Lansing, Chicago, even the Upper Peninsula—had permitted me a way to go somewhere, the first phase of many routes, what my mother considered . . . abandonment. The word rises unbidden.

Marie chimes right in, "You hear all those howls in your neighborhood through the nights; you know which one is which. You listen for the one that's not howling, that's the one gone bad."

Natalie agrees. "The roosters know. That's when they let go."

I'm stunned. The neighbors can guess which dog is breaking in to the pen by its silence? The rooster can identify a threatening dog and warns? I grew up with chickens but remember none of this. "Well, I guess that's why they banned the roosters," I say lamely.

"But the price of eggs in the store, you know?" Marie says, worried about me. "You can't make a good biscuit or pancake without an egg. You gotta have your eggs so you gotta have chickens."

I can see it in their eyes. How am I managing? I don't exacerbate the issue by confessing that I couldn't make pancakes to save my life and my biscuits come from a tube. But yes, she's right, four dollars a dozen for organic eggs is highway robbery.

"Doesn't everyone have some chickens?" Natalie asks, frowning.

"Not in a village. The chicken owners had to take the issue all the way to the village council, and they almost banned chickens entirely, but then they compromised and made the rooster ordinance."

"An ordinance?" Natalie asks, incredulous.

This sounds absurd even to me. I nod, say, "Only hens."

They look at each other, chuckle, and my mother actually laughs. Then Natalie of the lost thirty-first leans in and says, "What do you call a rooster who wakes you up at the same time every morning?" She's looking at me and Mom. No clue.

"An alarm cluck!" She slaps her knee. Marie gives a dark snort.

I think Mom will be embarrassed that she can't follow, feel left out, but she shakes her head sadly, "Not with just hens."

She's tracking. Then.

"Well yes, they are layers, not crowers," Natalie says deliberately, and they all chuckle again, and I can't tell if it's an off-color joke or pun or the togetherness of a small superiority they have created, but suddenly they know so much more than the village council, so much more than I do, and they are so subtly smart. I didn't see it, didn't know they could still think like this. These women, none of whom really understand what day it is, see the absurdity of the rooster ordinance. And my mother is right in there with the play on words. The moment shines like sun on those morning eggs, a scrambled gold.

And then of course Natalie asks, "What day is it?"

This time, when Marie tells her, she adds, "Good to know, huh?"

Natalie says, "Well, yes, means September's next."

No one corrects her.

Everyone's hair lifts a little, and all three women lift their chins and turn to the breeze, and as they do, their faces cool at last. The breeze is a thing full of their youths, their sprawling farms, a house in the open fields, a hutch with chickens. I watch Mom raise her head, greet that wind, in consort with it. The breeze is a July 31 breeze, and even here in the Manor, under the gazebo, it carries the scent of earth and harvest, the memory of making meaning from the land. These women strode open earth; their bodies remember the work, and their minds too, if given the context, if given something to lay into, the whole purpose of being, to gather the eggs, let the broody hen brood and the rooster protect. Now, their feet are swollen. They aren't sure what day it is. The rooster, gone. But they know the value of eggs, of those hens and a single insistent rooster. The two women push themselves up and head, wobbling gently, toward the door.

Mom goes quiet, staring at the medical care facility. No one mentioned the one unanswerable chicken enigma. What came first, the chicken or the egg? What comes first, knowing her for who she is, this woman of time and land who now is changing. Or perhaps I am the one who is shifting in this landscape, coming to know some things that I didn't think I would, coming to ask the why questions about us.

Mom asks her own. She points across the fence at the medical care facility, "Why do people go there?"

Because they are too frail or sick to stay here. Because their minds can no longer crawl inside a living breeze, inside a small joke and know what it means. Because a daughter won't take them in.

But I say, "There's just no place else to go."

AS LONG AS I KNOW YOU

The question hovers, pressing down, making its unanswered self a nuisance. I need to ask. And soon. She is dozing, her body in slump. Every time this happens, I wonder if she's slipped away.

"Hey Mom, I'm here." She raises her head, eyes sullen. I adjust the chair, her body. I speak too loudly, using my cheerleading voice, not that I was ever a cheerleader. *It's a beautiful day, all that sunshine, have you been out, did you play bingo, what was for lunch?* She answers none of this. She looks at me with passive and uninformed interest. I am someone she knows, maybe likes, but ... then suddenly, "Oh, Anne. Well. Well. So good to see you."

I've brought roses and an apple. Ridiculously bright magenta and yellow blooms, and an oversized Pink Lady. The roses look droopy, the apple's soft; she looks tired.

I fill a small tub of warm water in the bathroom, bring it to the chair. I lift her hands into the water, and she swirls her fingers, awed, almost spilling. I wash her hands, fussing about the nails, *You got snacks under those?* I make a ruckus of looking for the clippers, this to bother her awake, and also so she can keep her hands in the water longer. We are children of water. Even she; it wakes us.

I lay out the nail-trimming tools. Though her skin is dry, her nails are long and fast growing. She lifts her hands from the warm water, lost to the pool dripping onto her afghan. We both stare at these nails that grow naturally into a perfect taper, this physical anomaly, nails that contradict the life of a farm woman, lifelong gardener. She speaks at last. "Boy, those are long." She's coming back. We echo to each other, *Boy those grow fast. Boy those are long, will you look at that?* I trim and file slowly, stretching the time. She makes humming sounds. Is this the first time today she has been touched? Of course, aides touch her to transfer her, to change her Depends. They wake her, get her up, help her take pills. Clinical and swift: touch reduced to professional purpose. But to be touched for the purpose of touch, so touch can do its work, so touch just might wake her to the question—no clue.

So, I press her hands into water, which does its good, rousing her. She flicks her fingertips.

"Stop wiggling. Just like Tom." Tom was my restless little brother, always splashing in the tub. She cracks a smile.

When I finish scraping, she asks, "Did you get it all?"

"Yup, but you could root a tree in that water." Another grin. I rinse and dry her hands. Then cream, buttery and soothing. She admires her shorter nails. "That's better," she says softly. Suddenly, she looks at me, aware and sharp. "Where have you been?" Accusing and querulous, she's awake.

Two libraries, four bookstores, a wedding, a book launch— eleven different beds in the fourteen nights I was gone. I've talked too much, slept too little, driven too far alone. I tell her. She looks out the window—ignoring me, or just bored? The old pattern: lives lived too far apart. She sees the starlings, glossy and greedy, raiding the bird feeder. "Look at that," she says, as if the birds were the important thing. Maybe they are.

I need to ask the question.

I pick up the apple. Hold it to her. She nods. The corkscrew blade cuts rough wedges. I have come to this: carrying a corkscrew in my handbag. I hand her tiny apple bits. We sit like this: Eve and her daughter long after the fall—camaraderie and regret, sharing and loss, filling up on all those apples from the tree of knowledge. She chews slowly.

On top of all the travel, I have been learning about this thing called caregiving, and more precisely about its corollary, how we die.

There are some seventy-seven million of us boomers alive, and some forty million of us are already doing serious care of an adult in some form. Mom's a frail ninety-four. I'm a robust sixty-plus. Some days, I think she can't hold on much longer, that she will slip away like fog anytime. Some days I think she will be one who lingers and lingers all the way past the centurion mark, beyond her children.

So, this question, academically expressed but about as academic as an apple—is about how she wants to die, and its corollary, the quality of life she wants while she lives. Mortality is what we are talking about here, and I am trying to figure out how to approach it with Mom. She does not easily speak of death.

Atul Gawande in his book *Being Mortal* writes that we have to ask each other what gives life meaning, what matters in the actual living. For some people, that's chocolate ice cream. For me, it's writing, or any creative act. For Mom? She's finally signed all the right papers, taken care of the business end, but I have never asked her this. *What makes her daily life worth living?* What I know: even though I helped create this life in which she is living, I would be hard-pressed to live as she is living now. *Judge Judy*. Bingo. Canned pears. Starlings at an empty feeder. Boredom. Loneliness. We made her safe, so she could stay alive, but what makes her *want* to stay alive? I hand her another apple wedge. She studies it. "Skin is tough." Out-of-season apples, sprayed to keep skin intact. I decide to pare the skin.

I breathe. "Mom, I need to ask you a question," soft opening for a serious conversation.

She has a mother's sixth sense for alarm that never fades. It kicks in. She looks at me sideways, "What's wrong now?"

Use the slow on-ramp. "Mom, I figure you will live for a long time yet, but I want to avoid what happened when Dad died, us trying to figure out what to do if you were really sick and couldn't tell us what you want. And so, I wondered if you can tell me what it is that makes life worth living for you? So I would know that if you couldn't have that—whatever it is, I should let you go."

I expect her to scold me for bringing it up, tell me not to worry about her, that *it's in God's hands*, which it may well be, but I'm not trusting God all that much these days. But my master-of-avoiding-all-things-death mother answers like it's a second-grade question. "Oh, if I didn't know you."

I sit back. "So, if you didn't know . . . couldn't interact with people . . . ?" I want a more nuanced explanation.

"If I didn't know you, you kids, anymore." She nods to another apple slice, eager for the sweet now that it's peeled. "Long as I know you." She'd said it right the first time.

She has given my sister and me medical power of attorney, signed an advance directive—comfort measures only. But now. Does she realize how this changes who we are?

She turns to the glossy gold-flecked birds back at the perches. "What are those again?"

I reach for her hand, hold it lightly. "Starlings, Mom."

"Oh, that's right." She recognizes them. But knowing is different. Knowing hovers in another realm: the attention and intention one must muster to know a person, to honor with the eyes, voice, face, kiss, to act within this *knowing*. Signature gestures, tone of voice, scent of skin. This is what I'm asked to hold in place—the placeholders of identity. And we, now I know: we will not let her go easily. I split the last bit of apple between us, peeling some spot of toughness away.

WHISKERS

"Whiskers?" I look closely, bending over her blue recliner, trying to see what she's talking about.

"I can feel 'em." Her hand trembles at her chin. I peer. There they are, three long, downright wiry furies curling on her chin. A wild haiku of hairs an inch or so long. Then I notice a translucent dusting of beard across her upper lip and under her chin.

I've missed this. I pluck her eyebrows sometimes but never noticed her chin. Does it begin, this thin-stranded beard, when you've lived nine decades? All those whiskers whispering their wiry cronedom.

"Okay, I'll pull them."

I start with the tweezers. She winces.

"Does it hurt?"

"Not at all." She winces again.

"It doesn't hurt?"

"No." A little jerk of her head.

I sigh, step back, think. "Mom, do you have a razor?"

"Dad's electric one." Fifteen miles away, at her cold house on the river.

"What about a disposable?"

She thinks. "They take all that stuff."

Given the amount of trembling that goes on in this place, I figure that's probably a good idea.

"Mom, I'm gonna run to the drugstore. Buy one."

"Oh, don't do that.

"You'll feel better."

A long pause. "That bad, huh."

How the hell do I shave my mother's chin? I find myself asking these questions more often. How the hell do I . . . ? There is more and more that she can't do, can't remember how to do, or doesn't know that she needs to do. So, we (my sisters and I) assume this ungainly process of relearning an activity we do automatically for ourselves but have little idea how to do for her. We are not unwilling, but when it's your tough, critical, expectations-high-as-the-sky, strong-willed, bravehearted, no nonsense mother . . . ? Each of these events takes me by surprise, then grows its own hairy threat simply because I don't know how.

Razors. *Oh Lordy*.

Somewhere, I have seen an old-school illustration of a young boy at a barbershop, all soaped up in the chair, barber hovering over, straight edge in hand, poised. I have seen movie scenes from old Westerns of men being shaved by gossipy barbers wielding dramatic razors. Then there's Sweeney Todd, of course, that straight-edged madman, but let's don't go there. Not one equivalent iconic image or scene of a girl's first time shaving her underarms or legs. Unworthy of Rockwell's, Sondheim's, or MGM's attentions? And YouTube videos of a daughter shaving her elder mother's chin are as unlikely. What I do remember is that David, who shaves with a Gillette triple blade every day, still cuts his chin on occasion and enters the kitchen with bits of toilet paper stuck like tragic origami onto the scrape. The image that my mind conjures: her chin spilling blood and me trying to stop up a mortal wound with her superabsorbent pull-ups.

Against my environmental impulses, I buy pink Gillette disposables for ladies. I suspect, if I get through this, it won't be the last time I do this, but in between times, who will keep them clean—so it's disposables for now. I wash my hands, put a soft towel around her neck, soap up a paper towel, soap her chin, tear open the disposable, and turn to her, wielding the pink-for-ladies.

The hair is coarse and . . . I search for the word. Manly. Yes, these hairs are puffed up, defiant warriors. I place the pink-for-ladies against her chin and start what I hope is a smooth draw upward, as I would if I were shaving my legs. I tell myself: this shouldn't be hard. This is a small thing in the scheme of so many things that are just basic grooming. No big deal. But the whiskers whisper again. *You can't get us. We'll make your hand shake.*

I hate my imagination.

Focus. The folds of the vulnerable neck, the rounding chin, and her skin so thin. I move slowly. She closes her eyes. I press a little harder. How hard before I scrape the skin? Or pierce it? I stop, take a breath, and she opens her eyes.

"You can do it."

No caveat, no impatience. She did not warn, *Just be careful.* She did not say *No.* She gave permission, a quiet yes. I have to turn away, rinse the razor before I start again.

And one by one, the troublesome hairs go silent, cut down, drowned in the soap residue. With them, a thousand nos, as many lies. Soap, stroke, stroke, soap again, stroke, stroke. Chin done, now her upper lip. I soap her up again. When I pull the skin at the side of her mouth, she sticks her tongue into her upper lip so it bulges; it's easier to pull the razor over the tighter skin. How does she know to do this? Under her nose, a quick repeat, just to make sure. I run my fingers over, touching around her lips, mouth. I've got them all. I wipe her face, rinse, find moisture cream, apply it all over. Her face is dry and clear. I haven't cut her.

She rubs her chin, "Feels lots better."

Then she reaches out, grabs my hand.

How do I say this next part? She holds my wrist close in her fingertips, and pulls my hand against her face, and keeps it there.

"So smooth," she whispers.

In this moment, when I must do for her, and she doesn't like it, not one bit, her hands gently hold my wrist, my fingertips to her face. Here is touch, the tender blade she has allowed me to draw over her face, the thin skin between us for once without bristle. Here is a yes between us. But I do not know the woman who stands here, breathing next to her. In her rough assurance, in her touch, she has made me a stranger to myself.

ANN AND ELIZABETH

Passover. I'm invited to a friend's Seder, an honor for a Gentile, and I don't want to be late, want to be with my Jewish friends for their holy ritual, want to say grateful things, tell a grateful story. So, I'll hurry a visit to Mom at the Manor, take my leave, and arrive at my friends' home with time to spare.

In the long hall, I fall into step with Ann, a woman about my age. She's looking for her mother, Elizabeth. Over the long months, we daughters, a whole gaggle of us, have begun to recognize each other, to exchange friendly greetings, have become comrades in this journey. Our mothers or fathers are here. So we are here.

Most days, Ann's mother, Elizabeth, pushes her walker up and down the Manor halls, smiling, looking up, and asking her tender little questions in a kitten voice. *How do I get to my room? What are you doing? When will she come?* I've taken cues from the aides who always answer Elizabeth with their warm summer voices, even if they are making up the answers.

Just turn this corner.

We're eating lunch.

Soon, soon.

Ann asks Jennifer, the charge nurse, "Where's my mother?"

Jennifer speaks quietly. "She's around the corner." The long hall then. Then Jennifer adds. "She's using a wheelchair today."

Ann looks at her steadily, "That's new."

Though Ann and I usually chat easily, the wheelchair has startled Ann. She apologizes, moves quickly around that corner. I head to Sittercise because Mom is supposed to be there, all of the residents raising their arms above their heads, twirling their wrists like birds learning to fly. But when I arrive, she's not there.

I head back to her room, turn the corner, and there, again next to the wall, Elizabeth sits in her wheelchair. Ann is kneeling before her. Ann is looking up into her eyes. I slide past, moving quietly around them. But Mom's door is closed and from the muffled sounds of protest, the aides are changing her. She doesn't like me with her when they do that, doesn't like it done at all. I have to wait, so I try to become invisible in a folding chair next to the potted plants, but I cannot help seeing Ann and her mother. Ann kneels in front of Elizabeth. Elizabeth says one tragic line over and over, "I don't know who you are. I don't, I don't . . . know . . ."

Ann's face is drawn as tissue.

Is it the first time? I would like to shout at Elizabeth, to punch something. This stupid Alzheimer's, dementia, stroke, aging—this break-your-heart process. I want to leap to Ann's side, insist on her name, but I'm paralyzed by this mother-daughter drama that will not brook a breach of privacy, even though it's occurring in a public hallway.

"Who are you? Who are you?" Elizabeth's kitten voice mews.

Ann is quiet. She drops her head almost to Elizabeth's knees. I want Elizabeth to reach out and touch Ann's graying hair, to say, *Oh there you are, my Ann, my daughter Ann*, but Elizabeth shakes her gray head, mutters in quiet panic, "I don't know you."

She's your goddammed daughter, and you better recognize . . . that would be so effective.

Then Ann lifts her head, looks at her mother, and says the holy thing. She says, "You're Elizabeth. You're Elizabeth."

And Elizabeth slows, stops trembling, nods, plucks at her blanket, nods some more. She claims her name softly back, "I'm Elizabeth."

"And you're my mother." Ann's voice is steady.

Elizabeth nods again, and they look at each other, nodding.

How did Ann know the real question was not *Who are you?* but *Who am I?*

My eyes blur; I can't watch. I break the rule, knock on my mother's door, and barge in. She is still in the Hoyer lift, swinging in the huge blue sling that cowls her head like a monk's habit while two aids surround her, overcoming her resistance. It's crowded and smells. Swinging wildly, Mom still sees me and promptly scolds, "Well as usual, Anne, you came at a bad time."

Oh Mom. Yes, a bad time, and I'm staying because even though I can barely see your face, I would recognize that butt hanging out of that sling, and even though you asked me never to come when this was happening, you knew who I was when I walked in. And you know who you are.

Do I love her in that moment? I do indeed.

The first question of Seder. *Why is this night different from all other nights?*

Today, I watched another adult daughter love her elder mother better than I imagined possible. I saw what a daughter could do, how a daughter might see the real question, might set aside her own need to be seen. I saw how it could be done, how a mother who had lost her self could be given back at least her name, led out of the desert of loss. The angel had passed over, leaving me, the firstborn, with new knowledge, a bitter herb. I must taste this knowing. I must know myself so when the time comes, I can know her back to herself.

I have no idea how to do this.

THE LAST VISIT

In that afternoon light full of river and late summer air, we mean well. We mean no harm. We don't mean for memory to do some dirty work.

Pat's home, visiting from Colorado. We have escaped the Manor with its long hall, brought Mom out to her remote house, out here to the country of river and autumnal leaves rushing in September sun, all this before we finally clear the rooms of the identifying furniture, before we dismantle this final piece of her life. The light bears witness, the light gathers into bundles in the maple trees, exploding with the colors of betrayal.

We trundle her into the house, get her settled at the table. Pat makes salad, Marijo slices the last of her summer tomatoes. I set the table with flowers, which Marijo adjusts because she has the eye for that. The river light flickers on the ceiling, throwing ripples through the room. Marijo leads the blessing and we join hands and bow our heads and say amen and lift our heads. We smile and eat a hearty lunch. Mom keeps saying, "It's so good." And how much she loves real food. The food at the Manor is plain. We know this; we don't like it. But we don't say anything; we don't ask anything more from the aides who change her pull-ups twice a day, who check her heart regularly, who go out of their way for her. We eat with Mom, and we laugh as much as we can, and we try to keep it all happy this afternoon for her and her three daughters.

This last time. She doesn't know.

She eats well and we help her to the bathroom and we change her and we get her back out into the living room and we pull her wheelchair up to the window where she can see the river light. The light falls on her white hair, falls on her lap, where her bad hand rests in its arthritic distortion, falls on her twisted shoulder, eternally curved round like fruit past prime.

Anna, her neighbor to the east, knocks and comes in, open armed with welcome homes. Conner, hearty and loud from the west, does the same. They enter the house with their big voices, their big welcome. But not for long. No one can stand the odor for long. But they come, remembering the times. Always a pot of burned coffee on the stove, always the place bustling grandkids in and out. All the fish to fish from the river, fruit to can, mushrooms to hunt. The winters, the summers. The neighbors leave with fondness and quiet looks back; they know what is happening. They have seen the signs.

We ask Mom if she wants to look at old photos in the albums but she says, "It just makes me feel sad."

She does not enjoy nostalgia. I suspect too, a deep-seated regret, remorse she can't address, plain loss. It is gone, the time when she and Dad were the center of the family universe. So much is gone, and for all she has forgotten, she has not forgotten the sense of tribal wonder, the gathering and regathering of those beloved, from childhood to the moment Dad died. So, we sit in chairs near the window and watch the salmon run, the new ones, still strong, claiming the redds at this turn in the river. They are big and still pink fleshed. If you fish, this is when you want to get them. Now and then, they fight, splashing wildly, and she says, "Look at that."

Hoping maybe she'll offer more than fish commentary, I ask, "Remember way back, when we grew potatoes?" I'm thinking of their young farm, the beginnings. I have some brief memories. The cold wet fields, the dark soil pocked with the brown spuds. And then, in the house, a ratchety sound rises in memory, and a feeling in my feet. I ask, "Did we grade potatoes?"

"Dad had the grader in the basement, and they'd sort three sizes.

What a racket." Yes, that's it: sound and vibration rising up through the floorboards of the old farmhouse into my bare feet. "They stank," she says, shuddering.

"Nothing quite like rotten potatoes," Marijo says of potato odor, ignoring the present one. To remember those potatoes with my sisters and my mother is to remember in the presence of witnesses, is to extend memory, to open a moment from the past to experience in the present, to keep the connection with the past alive. I'm counting on that, despite what I now know is coming. "What was the farmhouse like when you moved in? Before we came along?" Late forties.

"There was a cistern in the attic."

We perk up. Then she says, "Some rats had drowned in it. We found them when we drained it. I said we couldn't use it. That's why we dug the well." She closes that door.

Pat goes further back, asks, "Your dad? Grandpa Joe, he raised wild birds, didn't he?"

She nods, "Pheasants." Mom thinks he learned about animals in the war. "He was good with animals."

"You think he could have been a vet?" Marijo asks.

She pulls herself away from the river, looking straight at us, "He wasn't schooled."

Marijo and Pat draw a blank. "He couldn't read." She says with annoyance. Then, "Life was just hard."

My sisters pause, pull back, don't ask.

I miss their look. I want this shared remembering, my sisters, all of us. "In what ways, Mom?" I press.

The list rolls off her tongue as though she had memorized it.

I wet my pants.

We used kerosene when everyone else had electricity. The smell was a giveaway.

We had lice. We gave it to the school. They were mean about that.

My teacher tried to help me by giving me little jobs, washing the boards, so I could earn money, but it separated me from the others. It made me lonely to walk home by myself.

I didn't have a slip for my one dress. My underwear showed though.

This from the woman who never talks about her past. Pat's face is wet. Marijo has gone quiet, holding Mom's hand. And then my mother says, "I did not have a happy childhood."

Everything is too bright now. Everything is standing out in that bold September light.

TEA LEAVES II

> In the use of tea-leaves as a means of divination, the more
> developed the "clear sight," the more interesting and accurate
> will be the interpretation. Practice is most necessary,
> especially for those who have less natural clairvoyance.
>
> —"Introduction to the Divination by Tea-Leaves," Divination by Tea-
> Leaves, http://divinationbytealeaves.com/introduction-to-divination-by
> -tealeaves.htm

As we finish clearing Mom's house, I have to go back again, return
to her life, her roots, reexamine the tea leaves yet again, try to dis-
cern some meaning of that lost childhood and how it came down to
her daughters, to me, to the ways we know each other, to the ways
we are strangers.

After that initial five pieces of Tea Leaf ironstone, she had ex-
panded the collection to include twelve dinner plates, ten luncheon
plates, an array of bread plates, several serving bowls, and a mix of
mismatched cups and saucers. I also realized: we never used them.
The nicer pieces were showcased in little stands, coppery luster
catching light. She had learned to set a beautiful table while working in that mansion in Chicago, but when we set our Sunday dinner
table, she demanded the chipped and cracked Wheat Harvest pattern from her wedding, never the Tea Leaf.

Sometimes she traded pieces with other collectors. I didn't pay
much attention, but I think she was good at it. She found articles in
magazines on the first makers of the Tea Leaf pattern, the Brits, and
learned that the Tea Leaf is rare in Britain because it was shipped

so heavily to American shores from the mid-1800s on. The iron-stone was tough and traveled well. Of the British-sourced pieces she would announce, "These survived the crossing over."

I didn't ask what she had survived. Not for a long time.

Later I learned the simple elegance of that white ironstone, just touched by the coppery trim of the leaf pattern, was the first "cultured" tableware available to working-class Americans who had previously relied on wooden bowls and pewter plates for standard tableware. I think about that, what it would have been like to set a table with creamy ironstone after years of dark wood or gray pewter. I imagine the pride of those early women, not over fine porcelain, but this sturdy ironstone, common but with that flash of coppery leaf gracing their tables. I think my mother felt a kinship with them; once she said, "These plates just glow on the table." But she never set our table with them.

Still, with each new piece, there would be a moment when it was washed and dry and smooth and glowing, and she would set it down before her, and study that coppery leaf, sometimes tracing with her finger. Once in a while, she sat with it. Stared at it. Evenings after things quieted—which happened rarely, she might sit at our table, place a piece in front of her. Was she reading some prophetic future in that emblem? Trying to assess the value?

What I learned slowly over time, from the old photos, from half stories that I confirmed with cousins, with aunts and uncles: parts of her life were set in stone, stilled in fire.

> In the case of tea-leaves, where the symbols are not mere "conventional signs" or numbers but actual figures like the pictures seen in the fire or those envisaged in dreams, there is no doubt that the signification of most of them is the result of empirical experience.
>
> —"Symbols Explained," *Reading Tea Leaves: Guides and Info*, http://readingtealeaves.org/alphabetical-list-of-symbols-with -their-significations

The first fire, 1932. By then, Grandpa Joseph had a grand barn on that good plot of land in Elbridge Township. The Van Agtmaels were doing well. There were work horses, a matched set, proud and strong

Belgians, after our heritage, the sturdy ones that could pull through a spring mud like it was sand. He housed them, along with other farmers' work horses that he was training, and the cattle, in that new barn with the threshing machine. But it was the horses, those grand Belgians, that my mother remembered.

"Handsome animals, real workers and strong, but not very smart." She shook her head.

The fire started in the mow, worked its way down. Winter, cold, wind, and all of the horses caught in the lower levels. Joseph went in through flames, grabbed hold of those big panicked creatures, led them out. But in the ruckus, he did not or could not tie them. Or maybe they broke their ropes. They are, as Mom said, sometimes stupid. While he was chasing the cattle out the back, the horses raced back into the barn, a place they knew was safe. The only place not safe. He went back for them, but my mother said simply, "They perished."

He had no insurance on the barn, only the house.

He rebuilt, borrowing all he could, and this time, he transferred all the insurance to the barns. Clearly the barn was the important building. Is that also when his drinking escalated?

Imagine two years later, Grandma Julia, canning in the old kitchen of their farmhouse, a kitchen like every farmhouse, never updated, never maintained for safety, never modernized with a new stove, ignored for that more important barn. Had she been canning all day on a cookstove with good wood sending its waves of heat and sparks up an old chimney? No one knows when a chimney fire catches because it's invisible, a secret inside the bricks or mortar until it escapes and proclaims, a sudden singing, darkening across the ceilings, smoke spilling down, a room gaudy in the orange gauze of overhead flames.

Mom was visiting the Indians, native neighbors who lived across the road, when the alarm went up. She had liked to play with one of the older girls, whose name was Jean, from whence came her own middle name. The call came and she went running. The family had time to haul out some things, but the house was a loss. A photograph of the smoldering remains, a few timbers still standing, the front porch thrust out like a tongue from the ashes, the front lawn strewn with pieces of furniture and boxes of kitchenware, grayed and gaping.

Mom wouldn't talk about the fires—what she said was like listening to a headline without the feature. *The house burned. We saved a few things.*

Grandma Julia had talked—I remember that—about precious things in a house that I always thought could not afford the precious: a porcelain doll, three beautiful hats, one graced with peacock feathers, a family cradle made of oak, a tiny child's rocker. In one of the boxes on that lawn must be the five pieces of Tea Leaf, grabbed on the run, dumped unceremoniously. Is that why the pieces are so chipped, cracked with the spidery alphabet of heat damage? Is that why the brown shadows like dirty clouds?

After the house burned, the family moved into a tiny place without plumbing or electricity, a mile away from where the new barn stood now isolated, fully insured and safe, but without its partner house. Julia and Joseph and their children, Ruth, Robert, and Neil, lived in that small house for a long time. Mom remembers geese and ducks, pheasants and roosters running wild in the burdock behind the outhouse. She remembers her father making hard cider and playing cards in a shed.

The burned farmhouse was rebuilt and eventually went to Robert, the son who would make the farm the success it should have been. Joseph and Julia lived at the Croff Farm, now remodeled, plumbed, and electrified, until Joseph died in 1961 in his late sixties. He had finally quit drinking, but he smoked heavily, unfiltered Camels, until the day he suffered the massive stroke that killed him a week later. Julia was once again devastated by the kind of grief that debilitates like heavy snow—she could not move. That was when she came to live with us on our farm, the farm Mom and Dad had well established by then. At first, she came only for the winter, then year-round until about 1980. Mom said, "I couldn't lift her anymore." Not because Grandma was so heavy—though she was plump—but because her hip was fused, and to lift her was to lift dead weight. Mom couldn't do it alone with her own bad back. My mother had no idea then the choice she'd have to make eventually about her own mother.

> After a cup of tea has been poured, without using a tea strainer, the tea is drunk or poured away. The cup should then be shaken well and any remaining liquid drained off in the saucer. The diviner now looks at the pattern of tea leaves in the cup and allows the imagination to play around [with] the shapes suggested by them.
>
> —J. Gordon Melton, ed., *The Encyclopedia of Occultism and Parapsychology*, 5th ed., vol. 2 (Farmington Hills, Mich.: Gale Group, 2001)

As my sister Marijo and I pack Mom and Dad's river house, as we immerse ourselves in the fractured process of sorting, we move around the original five pieces of Tea Leaf ironstone like they are oracles of pain. We set them out, put them away, shift them in and out of cupboards, on and off countertops. I study not the pattern but the shadows on the platter, the coffee pot, stains like thin smoke. After the fires, was she ever again safe, or her loved ones? Not the flames but the shadows of flame haunt me, questions I cannot answer clearly but fear the answers I can guess.

> The answer, of course, is that the meanings given to the symbols are purely arbitrary and that there is no scientific reason why one should signify one thing and not another.
>
> —"Symbols Explained," *Reading Tea Leaves: Guides and Info*

Of the Tea Leaf, Mom says finally, "Divide them up, just don't fight over them." But as we packed, my sister Marijo and I can't do it. We can't lay claim, can't assign. Even the perfect one, the glowing compote, the pedestal of elegance. We'll put them all in storage.

One day, after Mom's been at the Manor for a while, I stumble on a complete set in an antique shop. I mention to the elderly proprietor that my mother collected Tea Leaf china, and from him I discover the vagaries of collecting. After a sharp rise in prices in the eighties, interest in this pattern fell. It's worth now only about what she would have paid for it. But in the course of the conversation, I mention how fun it is to think about tea readings associated with the pattern. The proprietor raises an eyebrow, says, "That Tea Leaf pattern ain't the tea leaf of the Asians."

"It's not?" Something crumbles in my mind.

"Not Oriental at all." He fingers the dusty plate. "That's a strawberry leaf. Country folks made tea with strawberry leaves when they couldn't get real tea, maybe for the vitamin content, so that was the real inspiration. You compare it to botanical tea leaf, you'll see." The man taps the pattern on a platter, "Honey, it's just a stylized berry."

I lift the compote dish, twirl an extra layer of bubble wrap around it. No fortunes can be told through this collection, but in reviewing these pieces, some mismatched plates, I can divine the value of her ironstone. Before I pack away the compote, I stare at the leaf pattern. I wish we could have done it together, this simple collecting. No, I wish we could have done something, anything where we could have been equals, where there might have been real camaraderie, where I could have been a friend to her and she a friend to me. I stop. Can mothers really do that? Be friends with their daughters? Daughters, friends with their moms?

I look down and realize I've already shut and taped that box.

DYNAMITE

She and I have begun to make our way. Even I can see that. Glimmers of laughter, touch, some rough declarations of gratitude. And still, my betrayal continues. Sort. Clear. Stack. Mom's dusty kitchen is full of boxes sitting like squat security guards. I'm breathing dust that should be sampled for an archeological dig and wrapping endless clutter when Marijo bursts in the front door. Marijo has been cleaning Dad's storage shed behind the house while I pack this stuffy kitchen. Marijo says, "I think we have a problem." Marijo is a problem solver, and she's good at it. So, if she thinks something is a problem, it is a problem. "Come look," is all she says.

She's out the door, long striding through the unmowed grass and pines, past the storage shed, headed to Conner's, the house right next door. Conner's our crazy, big-talking neighbor whom my dad adored, my mom put up with, who speaks with a gravelly voice, and has a fierce interest in all things weed. He has a perfectly legal medical card and is growing a handful of gorgeous plants in the backyard. We don't know if my father was ever aware of Conner's lifestyle, but I suspect that if Dad did, he was advising Conner on fertilizer use. What we appreciate is that Conner looked out for Dad and Mom, made sure Dad didn't have to plow his driveway in the dead of winter, checked on them like a good friend.

Con's an old hippie with health issues of his own. Why has Marijo gone to get him?

Within minutes, both are back at the storage shed, where she has partially opened the old hinged doors, tilted as tents, gouging the grass. I join them, staring into the unlit cavern, just as I hear Marijo ask him, "Do you think that's what it is?"

They are not entering the shed.

Con says, "I never seen the real McCoy, but if I were to guess, I'd say yeah, that's what it looks like."

She turns to me and asks, "Do you know why Dad would have dynamite?"

Dynamite? In the shed?

Then Con is saying. "Until you know, you might want to close those doors real careful like and just not breathe for a while. Do not disturb and all that."

Right on, Con. But this old building is disturbed and disturbing. Periodically the trumpet vine nailed to the back weights down with bloom, yanks out the wall anchors, and pulls down roof chunks as it falls. The roof leaks, and the siding is pocked with rot. And now—dynamite?

I slide past their bodies so I can see what they see, and there on the highest shelf, barely visible in the dim light, resting on heavy but decaying brown paper, eight sticks, faded red, the size and shape I imagine for dynamite. The sticks are bulbous with moisture and tiny crystals. I can just make out the faded "warning" and "fuse," a skull and crossbones, other words, blurred by age. Shit. If it has a fuse, does that mean ... ? I back slowly out of the shed, making sure not to jostle the rusted implements.

"How long does dynamite stay ..." I search for the word.

"Stable?" Con's face screws up in thought. "The shelf life of nitroglycerin? No clue. But that much, the whole place would go."

The shed sits six feet from the back of the house.

Marijo lifts one broken-hinged double door and with precise care pushes it into place, closes and latches it. She looks at me, and the question enters our heads simultaneously. *Why would Dad have dynamite?*

When we voice this to the man of the hour, Con throws his hands out, palms up. "I dunno. You better let Tom and Rick know."

Tom and Rick, our brothers, run Oomen Farms, where we all

grew up a few short miles away, the farm that my father and mother ran from 1947 until 1983 when it became incorporated. Mom and Dad retired here mideighties. From that small farm my brothers built an operation that is known throughout the region. It's so big, their base campus is the size of Dad's first asparagus field—five acres. Dad had continued to work on the farm almost every day, working as though it was still his, even though it was now his sons calling the shots. Though they were creating a success, he shook his head at their progressive "risks." Dad was a cautious man. So dynamite seems especially out of character.

Every well-planned betrayal has the potential to backfire in a cloud of debris. But really, dynamite? Marijo asks, "Isn't the stuff outlawed?"

Con grins, "Like since the seventies. Federal."

Dad kept an unstable explosive and broke federal laws?

Con's right, this is not something to handle on our own. This is a family affair. I text Tom: "Found what may be dynamite in Dad's shed. Can you check ASAP?"

We head back into our parents' house and Con heads home, hollering over his shoulder, "If I hear a big noise, I'll know what happened." He laughs.

Marijo and I look at each other. Marijo says, "That shredded paper means those sticks have been there for years." She chews her lip. I bite my nails. Finally, she says, "Oh, let's put on our big-girl pants."

"Meaning?"

"If it's been there this long, not likely gonna blow today."

Back in the house, we trundle down into the musty-smelling space where two dehumidifiers run, their soft hum covering the skitter of mice. I attack Dad's work bench, looking for stuff to sell at the garage sale, the first step to getting to the next step, which just maybe is preparing the house for a renter. Or sale. Mom wants to come home; we both know that. She wants out of the Manor, as though the Manor were a prison. For her it is; she's ninety-four now but her old will rises tenaciously. We've found her at the door of the Manor, examining the heavy latches with an intent look on her face.

It makes us laugh. It breaks our hearts. Why couldn't we take care of her here? The question hangs, explosive in nature. Every time I think about it, my guilt grows.

Odd electrical stuff lies scattered over the makeshift work benches, fabricated metal, wire, old tools. I start filling boxes willy-nilly but can't get the dynamite out of my head. "Do you think it's from the farm? Like maybe he moved it here from there?" I ask. I coil wire. How much heavy gauge did he need? My dad liked to put things together, not blow them apart.

"Why would he do that?" Marijo asks. She tackles the paint shelves, throwing spray paint into a heavy-duty bag. These she will take home to spray old lawn furniture in bright new-old psychedelic patterns. She's the most creative of all of us. "Wouldn't he get rid of it before they left the farm?" She's right; it makes no sense.

"Would Mom remember about dynamite?" Marijo asks.

I hit the call buttons. Once she finally answers, I can tell this is a good day, a day when she's speaking clearly and memory is still threaded to being. I get right to it. "Mom, do you remember if Dad might have kept dynamite in the shed."

No hesitation. "Oh, he might have."

Oh Lordy. "He might have? Really." I repeat this, as much to inform Marijo as to wrap my head around it. She pokes her head around the cabinet, all ears.

"Oh, probably not." Mom's voice goes far away. Did he or not?

"Why did you say that? That he might have." I hit speaker phone.

"Well, he had history with it."

History? Marijo mouths.

"With dynamite?" Something surfaces in memory: a sound.

Mom carries on, "He used dynamite way back, to blow up big tree stumps when he was clearing. Was . . . a big deal." She sighs.

Before she loses her focus, "But did he keep it? Around. In the shed?"

She comes back. "Once, he had a bunch in that old granary."

"At the farm?"

"He forgot all about it."

Marijo is staring into some shelf of mystery boxes, but at that, she looks over her shoulder, quiet alarm on her face. *He forgot?* I want to laugh. This was a man who won awards for safety, took his children to the basement in high winds. Marijo knows; he wouldn't forget.

"It was dangerous—he carried it over the north hill, put it on the ground. Then he took that big hunting rifle, lay down on the ridge, and shot into the dynamite. Exploded it."

"That's how he got rid of it?" Marijo speaks this aloud, as appalled as I am.

Then this tidbit. "Singed his eyebrows and gave him tinnitus for weeks." With that, whole and intact, a lost memory returns: his face red and without eyebrows. Yup, he had history.

"He was keeping us safe." I hear the catch in her voice.

"He just didn't want to lose the granary," Marijo says, almost loud enough to carry. Farmer humor. But when I press, Mom can't remember anything about dynamite at the river house.

Suddenly, "I don't want you girls messing around in there," she says. "You'll get tetanus, and then what'll you do?"

Tetanus? The least of our worries. But she's tired of talk, starting to slur. Being able to confirm "history" has not been reassuring. We sign off.

"We know this much. He knew how to get rid of it." Marijo grins wryly. She holds a jar of loose marbles that was stored, for some unknown reason, with the paints. Pretty little worlds that we once played with. Keep.

"He couldn't do that now." Was that the problem? He didn't know how to ask for help? I'm holding a handmade tool, some weirdness for the sprinkler system. Keep with house. I move to small appliances, tackle the old popcorn popper, wondering if it would bring a couple dollars. But no cord. Trash.

He hadn't known how to tell us about Mom's mind either.

"Look inside," Marijo commands. Ah, she's right, the coiled cord, along with mouse turds. Wipe it out. Sell. I open another box. Crockpot. The third one so far. How many crockpots did Mom need? And the bread maker? Sell and sell. On to seasonal decor. I'm elbow deep in dried flower wreaths, at least four for each holiday, when

I discover the mice villages. They have shredded Christmas bows and Fourth of July flags in a warren of riotous nests rank with red, white, and green mouse confetti. Trash. Mom would be appalled, not at the mice, at the tossing.

I righteously announce, "Before I get to her age, if I get to her age, I'm clearing every last itty-bitty thing. We all have too much shit, and we should make it easier on everybody and just let the crap go." Marijo eyes me; she knows the truth. I'm as big a crap collector as the next person. But why does their crap have to be dynamite?

Sometime in that long afternoon, we open the old upright dresser and find Mom's scrapbook from nursing school. We've seen it before, but not for decades. Her picture is pasted on the first page. "So young," Marijo murmurs, fingering the image of Mom wearing her white nurse's cap. We both think she's beautiful before the ravages of . . . a life she may or may not have wanted. Despite dynamite right next door, we settle at the card table in the dark hum of dehumidifiers and turn the pages. The scrapbook covers her nurses training, including the handwritten post card from the director that says they have an unexpected opening in the fall class, 1942, and that she should come to the Mercy Training Hospital in Manistee as soon as possible. We flip pages, and both of us note that she had, at some point, removed all the references to the boy she was engaged to during World War II, who was killed in action. A pastiche of dried out medical essentials: pressed and cracked nipples, curved rusted needles. We open a tiny envelope. Fifty-year-old suture thread that Mom had twirled into a coil. What the two of them saved. Suture thread and dynamite? Something to pull together the edges of a wound, something to blow a body apart, our childhood in that setting. We don't speak these thoughts, that Mom's history, our history with her, became with each battle a kind of dynamite on the shelf. We aren't sure what to do to release it, her, ourselves. Maybe that was Dad's quandary.

Marijo and I sit in the basement in silence, staring at our mother's life. Then, for the second time that day, Marijo puts on those proverbial big-girl pants, gathers her will, dumps the scrapbook

back into the recesses of the cupboard. We muster muscle, haul another exercise bike up the stairs, wrestling it to the garage. Forty
bucks.

This is our mother in us.

Tom shows up with our nephew Jared. The big truck crunches onto
the driveway and they climb out, Carhartted, heavy booted, serious. As is the habit with farmers, they merely nod a greeting, even
though I haven't seen either in weeks. I am not to take it personally;
this is the way. Conversation is usually terse. At least at first.

"Where is this stuff?" Tom asks, and we lead him out to the shed
and carefully pull open one door.

"You just gonna walk in there?" I am suddenly petrified for him.

"You did."

"But we didn't know."

He's looking at me with that what-you-getting-at-now face.

"I just wondered if we shouldn't call someone." There must be experts, professionals who do this. Tom doesn't have to do what Marijo and I did, albeit accidentally.

Tom says, "Look, anyone I could call about this is dead."

Dead? "That's *really* comforting."

He laughs at last. "That's not . . . I mean, people who knew how to
take care of this stuff are as old as Dad was. They've passed."

Ah, so they lived through it. "But shouldn't we call someone? Let
authorities know?"

He looks at me like I'm crazy. "Can you see the publicity? 'Patri-
arch of Oomen Farms hoards explosives.' Picture federal agents in
hazmat suits." He shoots the you-have-no-idea look.

I shut my mouth.

And he walks into the shed, Jared close behind. Tom is tall, taller
than Marijo, much taller than I am, so he has a new angle on the red
sticks. "Open those doors wider." Light floods in. He studies the
stuff from above.

"It says something about fuses," Marijo tells him.

He nods, shifts to different angles, brooding. "Thirty-minute
fuses . . . ? Why would dynamite have a thirty-minute fuse?"

He looks back at us, face clearing. "These are ... flares."

"Flares?"

"You know, old-style warning flares like you put out if you have a breakdown on the highway or something. Burn for thirty minutes. That's what it means." He shakes his head. He looks at us. "Dynamite?"

Marijo and I look at each other. Shit. This will become ammunition for months of teasing ... *those girls thought that stuff was dynamite* ... We are relieved, and a little pissed. It'll become a family joke, and we'll be the butt.

He reaches in, gathers the flares into his hands without any nervousness at all. "Might burn pretty hot but they won't explode. Besides, they're past their prime." He picks one up, tips it, points to a tiny date, barely discernable, 1973. So, the dynamite turns into a flare, a call for help, to warn or alert. *Dad, you prepared for the wrong breakdown.* The one on the highway never came, but the one of your own life—that one arrived without warning. If he'd had the foresight, would he have warned us about Mom? No, the flares were placed on the shelf, stored away.

Tom carries the swollen red sticks to the back of his truck and tosses them in ... the debris of an old history, hauled away in the bed of a farm truck.

Later, Marijo and I walk over to Conner's and tell him the story—he laughs and says, "Totally awesome. Had you gals going." I remind him he was no help. Still, we give him one of my father's best fishing spears, found in the back of the shed, the most illegal one of all, with the prongs hand welded backward so that the fish, once hooked on the spear, has no chance of escaping.

POST-GARAGE SALE BLUES

Hard has been the getting rid, the ridding of goods even as we are riddled with memory with every crockpot we touched, right down to her claim: *This is a good box, we can use it.* Among those boxes, years-old taxes—way beyond the seven-year limit, plus financial and health forms, owner's manuals for every appliance they ever owned, registrations and guarantees. Hard finding, lost in the mess, the original title to the house. *Geesh, what else is lost among these pages?* Except for the title, all of this is packed in a garbage bag in my car, stuffed like an overweight whale.

Hard is the manager at Polk Road Storage rental handing us the contract for a five-by-ten storage space. We will pay the thirty dollars a month rental fee for as long as Mom is alive, if what remains will just fit. "My sister and I are sharing this. We need an extra key." I don't tell the woman that the stuff we are storing is all that's left of Mom's entire household, including the Tea Leaf china and the retro star crystal we could not figure out what to do with, that we will save (now we know) until she dies. Hard will be when, only then, we will offer it to the family, if anyone should even want it.

Beth, the manager, agrees to the extra key, and I drive around to the north end of the facility, to D-44, and open the empty space. Hard is how empty and cold, clean and dry. Hard is how small. Hard is the hollowness in my stomach because the house is empty. Hard is how, when Marijo arrives with her loaded truck, we are hard-pressed to understand why we thought we could get so much inside that space.

Hard is wishing it would all break. Wishing we didn't need to think about the value of these dishes, trinkets, crockpots. Wishing we didn't have to be here making small hard decisions about the small hard bowls that defined their small wealth. We want them both to be alive and to be together and taking care of each other. And their stuff. Forever. We want him back, quiet and reserved. We want her back, yelling at us not to track on the rugs we are right now wrapping around glassware, to *be careful with that dish, it was Great-Great Grandma's*. Hard has been this house-emptying, this dismantling an insignificant life that they loved deeply.

Hard lifting down the pallets Marijo brought, stacking them on the floor so if it should ever flood, there will be less damage. Hard hauling in Dad's gun case, filling the drawers of the better dressers with smaller boxes, and boxes of photo albums in the gun case like puzzle pieces. In the end, we riddle it all in and where once we might have high-fived, we fall into each others' arms with long, hard sighs. We have filled the space with this tangible stuff, but nothing fills our emptiness. We stand before the open door in the October cold. And then we pull it shut, slamming it on the concrete floor. We lock the door and double check, checking both keys work.

There's one more thing. That October night, Marijo and I burn their papers. She drags the heavy garbage bag, thousands of pages, out to the burn barrel in her side yard. It is a hard-cold, hard-cloud night and we are bundled in winter jackets. We stand in the dark and feed the yellowed sheaves into the barrel. The smoke is not sweet but chemical as sudden anger. Sparks fly up into the dark, a fierce hot fire erasing their past, chronicles of their money, balance sheets of their simple lives, years of taxes and receipts for every hard little thing from groceries to a new pump—which never worked right. This hardscrabble documentation, columns tallied month after month, roars and ashes the ledgers of their lives. We watch the pages curl in a delicate sequence, and under different circumstances it would be almost beautiful, page after page bright-

ening, the letters suddenly illuminated like souls, then collaps-
ing, some physics of immolation careening through the molecules
of Mom and Dad's canceled checks. Sometimes, the fire wants to
smother itself, to lose momentum; we've thrown on too many
pages at once, and when that happens, Marijo stirs the barrel with a
long pitchfork. Then, a rush of brilliance, shards flourishing to the
starless dark. On each rush, a reckoning.

We stand present to each other. I study Marijo, her hood pro-
tecting her hair from ash, and suspect this may be harder for her
than for me; her relationship with our mother was even more difficult, more fire full, and in some ways more attached: they are very
alike. Here's a story on that. In college, Marijo had a child out of
wedlock, a child she had wanted to keep, but she knew she would
need help to raise a baby alone and stay in school. She saw that my
parents had passed through that initial shaming—which was scarring to her—but in the end, they were willing to help her. Though
they offered, she also believed that this was their time, after all the
farmwork and child-rearing, their freedom from all the responsibility and hardship. In one of the most generous gestures of sacri-
fice I know, she could not ask it of them. Eventually, with immense
sadness, Marijo gave up the child for adoption. At the time, and
in real ignorance of what that would mean, I silently agreed, not
because I didn't want Marijo to keep her baby, but because I saw
it differently: where Mom was in her life, in the throes of a meno-
pause so furious it had brought us to our knees, praying we would
survive. What had been monthly headaches, nervousness, short-
tempered irritability turned into bleeding that was nearly hemor-
rhagic and mood swings that had spilled into unpredictable random rage. It was the seventies. Even then we didn't realize that
what Mom needed was help, real medical assistance, medication,
counseling—and perhaps she didn't either. Even if we had suggested, she would have refused—this is what women put up with,
she said, and offering it up to God was the only thing she knew how
to do. Thus, though she loved her daughter, hers was likely a compromised offer. Later, I realized that she would never comprehend
the full reason behind Marijo's decision. It would mar their lives

forever with a regret neither of them could forget. And later, it would draw them together in pain.

This is not my story to tell, but it is one story of many that hangs in the air with my sister and me as we burn the taxes. The light burns over us; shadows of memory flicker a leaf-riddled lawn. We could be Macbeth's witches, we could be dark minions come to earth, but we are plain and tired women burning our parents' rubbish and trying not to think what our history means.

Our mother's house is empty now, her stuff reduced to a hard five-by-ten storage space. She will never go back. We are coming to the end of this hollowing out, facing this season of incoming cold. This is the hardest place, this yard where we stand before the heat of those soft pages with their hard numbers, the net worth of their lives up in flames. We watch the pages shrivel in their brevity, the archive that we create if we are citizens of this world, all disappearing up in smoke. Finally, the rusty burn barrel is so hot and old that on one side, the fire burns through the lace rust of the old metal, and suddenly the top collapses onto itself like closing a telescope, the once impenetrable now burned through, spilling what remains of the smoldering checkbooks, receipts, invoices—all hot dust into the dirt. We let the fire die, stumble into Marijo's kitchen stinking of acrid smoke, and we drink beer fast and hard until at last we fall into hard-earned sleep.

Finally, in the barrel, the hard shapes turn soft, softer, turning to nothing. A history lost.

SNOWFLAKE

Two nurses bustle into the room to help Mom out of her recliner, where she has been napping all afternoon, and now into her wheelchair, helping her transfer, telling her to "cross your arms tight." One has her by the pants, and the other is in front, and they lift, saying, "Just pivot," and she says, "Just a minute, just a minute." It's hard on their backs. But yes, easier with two people. Lately, it has become harder to transfer her into the car for doctor's appointments or the now rare lunch out. They exit quietly and I take Mom's hand.

Mom's nails are messy with color, the polish slopped onto her knuckles. Some warm peachy tone. "Mom, look at that."

She huffs, "What a mess."

We find the polish remover, and I start to rub the polish off. "Who did this?"

And she says her own name as though it were someone else, "Ruth Oomen."

So, she's been painting too? Rich warm peach—one of her colors. I marvel that she found the polish, opened the bottle, removed the brush, and somehow got her nails covered. I wonder if she spilled on anything besides her own skin. Once her nails are bare again, I hold her hands for a minute. She touches the backs of mine. "Have you been painting?"

"Your living room is Snowflake; Marijo and I painted it."

"You didn't tell me." She's accusing.

"We do that just to bug you." Teasing.

"I don't want that color."

"You don't know that color, Mom."

"Snowflake. That's just white."

"Well, the room hasn't been painted in twenty years, Mom, and it's done now." Like so many things. When I get up to throw away the stained tissues, she knows I am leaving for another week.

In a voice full of stone, she says to the window, "I don't want to stay here. I don't like it. I want to go with you. I want to go home to that ... whatever that color was." She looks me straight in the eyes. "I shouldn't have to stay here."

It is a shock, to hear it in a tone that says she wants to fight.

We had counted on her being past all that. I had counted on complaints and criticisms, on resignation and some acceptance. Even on whining. I should have known better. I had not counted on these words, said aloud. *I want to go with you.*

"Oh Mom, oh Mom," and ignoring the odor, I sit in her recliner. *Oh Mom oh Mom oh Mom.* Her need, out loud in the air, a snake alive and twisting. We wanted to believe the Manor was the better way for her, and once there, the whole family sighed with relief. Her silence had covered the lie in bright snowflake white. But now she has said it. And all my bitterness about our past drifts away, and I think, *Yes, let's bring her home—the living room is even painted, we can rearrange the furniture.* I think, suspended like a moon on a thread into an idyllic image of us caring for her with gentility and some kind of dignity and all is love and wonder. Then with a rush, memory rises up—our knowledge of that personality, followed closely by my own—all my ambitions, my books and teaching and David and my books—did I say that, these things shrilling as loudly as her voice ever did. When that roar recedes we are alone again, and there is only her face and mine, full of terrible regret. I hold her hand, and I don't say a word, and she looks down and she doesn't speak either.

And then I stand and brush her hair for supper, and I turn the wheelchair toward the door, and say, "Okay, now you're beautiful, now you're just gorgeous."

And she says, "Fat chance."

I roll her into the dining room, a room, even on an autumn evening, too bright.

And she points to a man eating alone, and says, "I just don't like him . . ."

"Shhh, he'll hear."

"Don't care," she sniffs. "Just don't care."

I tuck her knees under the table where two Evelyns are sitting in silence. I tell the kitchen aids she wants French dressing on her salad. I walk out the door, climb into my car. I'm gasping hard as I drive north. All the way home, on and off, her face and my face are the same.

HER BONES

Of course, I was in Chicago, trying to write when it happened. I had decided to write about her, this mother of mothers, this one human being who haunted me like a ghost, who I had defied and defy still, and who I now wanted, in these final years, almost desperately, to understand, to like if not love. I wanted to find some peace about us, to write into the nature of us, into the nature of difference, into the nature of knowing. To shape some meaning out of the chaos of our past. The only gift I have, if gift it can be called, is my writing, and the strategy that seemed right for this endeavor was memoir, writing into the memories, making sense of the two halves of the world we had shaped together. So, I was in Chicago, writing. It was not going well. It was whining on the page. How many ways could I say she'd been mean. Well, hadn't she? But what I could already see, the thing I knew but was ashamed to say: I had been no picnic either. I had not been an easy daughter. I'd been mean right back at her.

Then Mom broke her leg, the right one, which she leaned on most, just above the ankle. No one was with her. So, no one knows how it happened. Lydia, the charge nurse, found her collapsed on the floor of 116, writhing like a snake, the Breezy wheelchair twisted on top of her. Later, we will wonder what possessed her to try a transfer without help. Then we don't wonder at all. She wanted to make a change from one state to another, and she didn't have the strength and she fell, pulling the wheelchair on top of her. What I imagine: her feet tangling in the afghan, or her leg trapped between the footrest of the recliner and the actual chair. In that cleft. She'd grab for the wheelchair arm, but it would slip and roll away from her, then sudden weight on old bones. The snap. We never asked how long she lay there; we are afraid to know.

The night it happened, the Manor folks called Marijo and ordered an ambulance, which whisked Mom to the hospital. Marijo waited hours for the orthopedic surgeon, pacing and uncertain. My brother Rick came, and anxiety raced through them both as they worried. Finally, the medical practitioners confirmed what everyone suspected—a bad break involving a difficult set.

I was not there.

I listened in shock to Marijo's calm but tired voice detail the situation.

Where I was? Chicago, like I said. Living in a charming third-floor walkup near Wrigley Field, the home of dear friends who had offered a personal writing retreat while they taught in Paris. I had flown there after I had taught the MFA residency in Boston. Now in these few days before student work smacked my inbox chock-full, I had intended to dedicate deep, long hours to this new project (the one now quickly going to shit), not to mention getting an urban fix in the city I loved: favorite museums, bookstores, and theater. But mostly to write. I'd worked hard in that old-style shotgun apartment and rich third-floor light, but the words felt like martyr speak.

On one of the coldest afternoons the Chicago winter had to offer, I did what desperate women in desperate straits often do: I went shopping. Shopping in January is an old and favored ritual taught to my sisters and me by our too frugal mother, who insisted that January is when you get the best buys on what you really need—no matter that the item may have been returned, damaged, is the wrong size, and will never be wrapped in a pretty bow.

I hit the streets, walked and thought and walked and found what I needed on sale in my size with tissue still tucked in the toes. By the time I returned to the dusk-edged streets to walk home, I carried a new pair of leather boots from one of the best booteries in Chicago.

I dodged piles of ice through wind gusts that could have knocked me over, but it wouldn't have mattered, I was nearly dancing. I had new boots, cool boots, boots for these long legs that came directly from Mom. Nothing like shopping to reset a mood. I would beat this literary uncertainty, write this Mom book with some insight about life and wonder and mothers and daughters in this time—and I would write it wearing very cool black Cole Haans. I victoriously threw open the apartment door, the cats scattered, and my cell rang. Marijo's number. I dropped the boots but still missed the first call because my fingers were too cold. I should have taken it as a sign.

Finally, my sister's voice. "Mom's broken her leg. Pretty badly."

Mom is 275 miles north. There is a fucking Great Lake between us. I am not there. Again. I stare at the boot box on the floor. Boots made for walking. Boots that signaled long travel and absence, and long strong legs. Boots that now mocked my confidence. Could anything make me feel worse in this moment than her breaking her leg?

When I finally arrive in the Manor, she is already back in room 116, in her chair, her leg cast and propped. She's awake, red-eyed, and pissed. After preliminaries: scolding, questions about my whereabouts, teary accusations, I manage to gain the floor. "How did you do this, Mom?"

She stops midreprimand, thinks a minute, says with perfect conviction, "I was painting the ceiling of the kitchen, standing right at the top of the cupboard. All by myself." It's the wrong memory, residual from the last time she painted her kitchen, shortly after she and Dad moved into their little river house. That time, she'd broken her wrist. Of course, in her mind, she had been doing something useful, something that needed doing, painting her kitchen. Working. That ceiling. And no one there to help her—guilt perfectly aimed at me. Probably justly.

She says, "I don't know what I'm going to do."

We don't either, but that line, that moment of throwing up her hands means that it's we daughters' problem, and she intends for us to take it on because we put her here. This is a different kind of re-set. This is my mother without direction.

I tell her she's going to heal. I tell her it will take five or six weeks, that's what the doctor has told us. In the meantime, the aides and nurses at the Manor will take on extra care. More monitoring of the room. We will double our visits. She gives me a look of dark venom that disintegrates into something else.

Guilt may be universal to many daughters, Catholics, and Jews the world over, but my mother had enhanced the skill, set a new standard. In the end, even as a grown-up in my sixties, guilt is how she called me home. But now that I'm here, her look takes me be-yond guilt, beyond defiance; her eyes are dark. We settle in for a sea-son of wintering in a cast the color of despair.

Five weeks later, we head to the doctor's office at the hospital. To take off the cast.

Mom has been angry, yes, but what's more concerning: her pain has not stopped.

"That looks bad," Pat, my Colorado sister says. She's studying the X-rays, the black-and-white shadows hung on the backlit X-ray lamps. Pat has flown back to Michigan to help out. In the last de-cade, she has become a striking Colorado woman, has found her place in those Rockies at elevations of eight thousand and above. She climbs fourteeners. She does yoga. She is strong, she can help, and her assessment is on the nose. Looks bad.

In the dimly lit room, Pat, the doctor, a nurse, I, and even Mom, all of us stare at the image of Mom's leg, the blue-white bone light shining on our faces. We stare as though it were a treasure but it's really appalling. Mom is looking up from her wheelchair, exam-ining the image with the same intensity. The orthopedic surgeon has revealed to us *why, why, why* Mom is still in so much pain. The white shadows on the screen show a jagged break. The two parts of the break do not touch but slide past each other, misaligned.

Her bones have not healed. Hell, they are not even set.

Dr. Leven explains to us, including Mom in the conversation, that if her bones were healing, we would see something fluffy around the break, like "bits of cauliflower." I love this idea, this fragment of metaphor in the midst of worry. But there is no fluff or anything remotely resembling even the smallest cauliflower floweret. Not only has it not healed, it has shifted off the axis where he set it five weeks ago. Even if her bones were healing, this is not the way one would want these bones to heal.

"We can't leave it this way," He states firmly. The shards are so unstable they might eventually break the skin, damage the muscle. He suggests surgery, pins and plate, perhaps a pin up the center of the heel to catch the bone and hold it. Pierce the heel and stabilize it until it can heal.

Surgery? My sister and I look at each other. We already know. Our eyes say to each other—*no*.

Still, we listen politely to the god of bones tell us how he wants to do major orthopedic surgery on a ninety-four-year-old woman who, though cranky as hell, is not strong. When he's finished with the almost exotic description, he stops, looks at Mom to see if she has heard. She is looking up at him so expectantly, with such attention and respect, with a small smile, that I realize she has not understood a word. But bless her, she is worshipping. He smiles in return.

I take a breath, thinking into this complicated decision. I tell him I've been reading about postsurgical delirium in the very elderly, how they sometimes don't come out of it. I've read—perhaps he can confirm—that it can exacerbate dementia. Of course, "Mom doesn't have dementia," I claim in front of him, but we don't want to create circumstances to invite it. What will general anesthetic do? What I don't say is that with the pain, meds, and lack of movement, the dislocation of self is growing like a cancer. And which of these two choices is worse, going forward with major surgery in a ninety-four year old, surgery that might take what mind is left to her and isn't guaranteed to work, or letting the break go in a brace, knowing she will always be in pain and will never walk again?

Pat's with me, "Is there any other way?" Both of us look at him with our sisters-united faces.

But he's worried about the pointed end of that bone, he's worried about piercing and infection and *more pain*. He shows us how thin the bones are even in the places where they are not broken. But then he does finally look at our faces. From Pat to Mom to me. And back. There is a long moment of silence. He decides to *poke around*. I love him for these words: *Let me poke around*. He wants to touch the break. I want to touch the break.

He gets out the saw. In this story of her bones, I did not expect the saw.

Here, a whirling dervish, a curve with silver teeth.

He holds it in his hands, this tool that will let him poke around.

We realize he is going to remove the cast. Right here. Right now.

I'm thinking she will need to be moved to a table, that we will need to step aside so he can manipulate this tool that will let him poke around. I'm thinking I should ask for a lift to swing her onto the table, to position her correctly so the leg may be examined, but he does something I have never seen a doctor do. He pulls the power source for the saw right next to him and picks up the saw, and he kneels before her in her wheelchair. This one endearing gesture, kneeling, holds all the earmarks of humbling oneself to ask for marriage, or kneeling to wash someone's feet, or kneeling in reverence. Mom leans forward to watch. She is a little in love with him.

And then he turns it on and all thoughts of tenderness vanish.

Here, the brutal whine of a precisely wielded instrument, the shrillness of mosquitos multiplied by a million, a blade designed to cut through stone-hard plaster. Here, the whir stirs up fine, almost invisible pink dust as he places the blade and it eats a straight line through the right side of the plaster. Pat sits beside Mom, holding her hand. I stand behind Mom, rubbing her shoulder, though truth be told, I'm uncertain if I'm distracting her or myself. It scares me, this sawing through to the inner sanctum of a bright cast, through a thickness to where her true skin lies, flaky and thin. But I can't look away. A second cut down the left, not quite opposite, so two cuts at angles from each other, cuts demarcating a piece like the single section of a banana peel, a covered snub-nosed canoe holding her flesh. There is no sign of pain; as fierce as it is, the saw's teeth sink only to the exact depth of the plaster.

The nurse hands him long skinny pliers, a spreader, and they slide it inside his cuts and pry open the cast in tiny increments. Gently, he lifts out the section. Beneath that, layers of batting cradle her bones. He removes some of the batting, slips his hands inside the slits between the cast and the skin, slides his fingers in and *pokes around*. Short seconds of touching. He sighs, looks up, studies our faces, looks at Mom. Speaks.

No healing evident.

A partial anesthetic, Versed or something like it.

Reset the bone.

An entirely different kind of cast.

Four or five months, maybe longer, before it heals.

But no pins, no plates.

No surgery.

It is not a perfect plan, but it is a plan we can live with, and what's more likely and important, so can Mom. The break will be realigned so that when the "fluff" of new bone starts to grow, it will grow in the right place. What I hear implied: she may never be able to bear weight on that leg again. But Pat and I nod, affirming agreement. A plan to live with. He places the banana section back in place. He wraps and wraps. Mom smiles widely at him. He grins back, tells Mom not to run any marathons. He washes his hands and shakes ours. He says he'll set up this procedure for next week. With her eyes, Mom follows the doctor out of the room.

I wanted to be the one to break open that cast and lift the piece and touch the two points of bone as yet disconnected, to feel what he was feeling, the aberrations that announced to his expert fingertips what the good doctor understood perfectly from those few seconds inside the broken shell. How to reset a bone. How to compensate for despair. She smiles: suddenly I want a reset for Mom and me; not just new boots, a whole new cast. And then she says, "Well that's enough of that."

Change is slow as old bone trying to grow new. It will be months before new cells evolve enough to bear weight. To bear the wait.

STARLINGS

My ninety-four-year-old, sweets-obsessed mother is not interested in ice cream, not interested in opening the Valentine's cards—she who adores mail—not interested in her birds. She is not even interested in scolding, even if given the opportunity—which I have done in numerous ways, today by trying to wake her. She has withdrawn into silence, a bedridden, fever-ridden silence. Room 116 now seems both crowded and empty: recliner empty of her body, swivel-style lap cart table empty except for rumpled tissues, two Kinkade-adorned TV trays—one that has collapsed twice since I arrived—empty. And the Breezy wheelchair, that now essential equipment planted right next to the hospital bed we've rented, where she lies now because she is wearing a heavy cast on her leg, is the emptiest object in the room, wheels silent, waiting for her weight. The aides have placed her wheelchair here in case she wants to get up, so it's easier to make the transfer. Are they kidding? The wheelchair is a pouting guest with its back turned, its Breezy brand raised as mockery. I turn it around, sit in it. And with that, I stop mind-yelling, hold her too warm hand, and try to make sense of what's happening.

Five days ago, the coughing commenced; her lungs wheezing and crackling. The nurse diagnosed her informally with pneumonia, and that nurse called our doctor, whose new office is a full forty minutes away, and since Mom couldn't make a car transfer for an

office visit, the doc prescribed antibiotics and prednisone. Marijo gave permission. Now it's days later and she has been refusing
food due to serious nausea—when is nausea not serious—and she
is also not drinking enough water to keep her body hydrated, and
she won't answer questions, and after a flurry of family phone calls
and texts, I am here to decide with Marijo (via phone) if we should
follow the recommendation of the charge nurse and take her by ambulance to the small local hospital in Shelby. What has complicated
this decision: her mental state is a fog. All her old and reliable fight
has drained away. She's dead weight when we try to move her. Is she
trying to become literal dead weight?

Out her single window shines Michigan's threadbare winter
sun. Her bird feeder too is empty, one pleasure that she still takes,
watching birds, but even if it were full, there would be no birds
lured in. When aides come to change her, she refuses to sit up, refuses to turn for them, and so the lift gets rolled in, and she retches
as they change her, and when that indignity is over, she refuses all
but the merest sip of water, which makes her gag. Her breathing
is labored, though her heart rate remains just in the normal range.
She is sweating, but her skin, clammy. She slurs that there's a terrible taste in her mouth, then closes her eyes.

I make a wild guess. This old woman, despite what I suspect may
be an actual will to give up and die on us, has a very tough body.
Her body, despite all its issues, like most living creatures on earth,
is not giving up easily. The body is doing its work, going about its
business, maintaining its vitals despite illness. But the mental giving up, I discover, is a harder thing to understand, harder than flu,
pneumonia, incontinence, and being confined to bed. Giving up, if
that's what it is, should be a devastation of will, but for someone
whose will was so amazingly powerful, this is like trying to break
rocks with a nail file. Some part of her may want to be done; she
may be so sick that she would rather withdraw from life. But now,
her body won't let even that powerhouse will have sway, or not
completely. My mother may be trying to die, but her body is not
cooperating.

I have a bad moment there in her wheelchair. How to understand this, how to set aside my resentful girl-child who was always aware when the silent treatment was happening because silence was a shout in my head: I was not good enough and would never be, am incapable of any accomplishment shy of picking up lint. It takes a while to get past that.

It returns slowly, the criteria for her life. What she said: *As long as I know you.* Here, a first test, a first-time application to a life situation. With a variation, a question I did not anticipate: what if she doesn't want to know us, doesn't want to keep wearing this cast of recognition that molds our brokenness, our knowing each other?

"Mom?" I shake her arm. "Mom?" She does not respond.

Suddenly another layer of fear rolls over me. Is this really how I want her to die? Because if we let this go unattended, it will be a long and hard death.

And then thought goes one step further down this end-of-life rabbit hole, that inevitable spiral of unknown timing. Do I want her to die so I can be through with this time that I didn't think would ever happen to her, to all of us who are trying to figure out how to be good daughters and sons and who want, because we all have these pasts that are both silent and too loud, we too want to withdraw? There is some true inkling, hard as it is to admit, in this. But then it does not hold. I know myself just enough to know this: I will never know myself in any real way if I walk down that road.

Why does love have to be so difficult?

"Mom," I say louder, more insistently. "Mom!"

She slowly turns her pale face toward me. Stares for a minute before her eyes drift closed. Usually I say, *Hi Mom, it's Anne.* So she knows. So I don't have to face the inevitable. I want to say my name. I don't. Will she still know me? "Mom, it's me."

She opens her eyes. "Oh." A flash ... some glimmer. At last. "Anne." The mouth changes a bit, softens? Or hardens? Changes. It's enough.

As has been my practice my whole life, I defy her will. I decide I'm cooperating with her body. I lift the phone, call Marijo, who as

usual, is way ahead of me and has already arranged for the ambulance. When I get up from the Breezy, the starlings have returned,
raiding the husks beneath the feeder for what sustenance the other
birds have missed. They always come, always believe that there
might be something left.

BLOOM

We realize it's there; we can smell it. Oddly sweetish, reminiscent of decayed lily. What we wanted to heal had festered, organic matter now closed in, trapped, dying. First symptom, a rising stain on the graying cast, that vast below-the-knee to above-the-toes fibrous landscape that wraps the deep interior break just above the ankle. This is the second cast, the one after the procedure of resetting, the one that has been on for months. A small island surfaces, seeps up, dark bloom from the underside of that hard plaster, flower of infection.

I had been traveling, had been in Detroit for work on the new book, trying to decipher marketing, promotion, how to launch this peculiar memoir about, of all things, a decade in 4-H clubs. I had taped a morning show of *Ideas Live*, a public access TV show I cohosted. I had been on Stateside radio, and now was full up with head-list to-dos. Mom had recovered from her pneumonia, and we were on our way to that famous cauliflower. So I thought.

I opened my emails. Bobbi's popped up. Bobbi is one of the clerical staff at the Manor. The email read: "I just wanted to run a couple things by you regarding your mom and her cast. The girls have noticed that the small wound under the top of cast may be oozing more, possibly causing a smell but with definite drainage. The cast itself also has a horrible odor that the girls noticed this week. Not sure if we have an infection going on in the skin under it or if it's just getting hotter and the cast is smelling. Spoke with Michelle at Dr. Levin's office and she states she can get in sooner if we go to Muskegon, but I know it's hard with transportation. I also wondered about having Great Lakes Care evaluate the wound at the top of the cast. Please let me know what you think."

Draining? Odor? Great Lakes Care? What I think? I think we need to get her to a doctor today. A dozen phone calls to his office, half a dozen messages for Marijo later, I cancel everything, climb into the Fit feeling totally unfit, and head for the Manor, trying not to think about the fact that I was supposed to take her in for assessment the previous Thursday. I didn't. I had been in Detroit. I had driven to the press to breakfast with the women there whom I think the world of, who can help me sell this book in which my mother is no small figure. If I figured anything at all, I figured she'd have a few more days to grow cauliflower. What kind of daughter am I to think a cast that's been on for months can wait?

An arrangement surfaces: Marijo and I will accompany Mom to the emergency room in Muskegon the next day at ten using the ambulance as transport. Dr. Leven will leave surgery, do the assessment, make recommendations, return to surgery. I didn't know this was possible, to use the ER like an office visit, the ambulance like a handicap bus. I wonder what this will cost us, we who think about her money and how little is left. I keep my mouth shut.

I arrive at the Manor at dusk, time of slow birds and long shadows but I barely notice. For the second time in a season, I stand at her window and watch her feverish sleep. I want her to wake up so I can be reassured, so I can tell her I'm sorry I didn't do this last week. In the dull spill from the window, I know it's no time for her to reassure me. Forgiveness is not her problem. We were never good at it anyway. But for me, the guilt is piercing.

I force myself to notice that her breathing is regular and her pulse, when I take it, fast but steady. Then I do what I have come for: with great caution, I lift the pink bedspread, pull back the sheet, and study her leg in this now all-wrong plaster. Her toes are swollen and white, almost hard—little circulation—but there, at the top of her arch, the irregular, reddish-brown of old blood, the stigmatalike bloom rising in chalk desert, small really, about the size of a half dollar with shadows under the surface. It smells. Like a dead flower.

Later, I have to be calmed by Lydia, the second shift nurse. She assures me: *Yes, your Mom's fever is actually down, broke just before she fell asleep.*

Tylenol worked.

She's okay for now, and you have an appointment in the morning—her vitals are normal, go to Marijo's and be ready for tomorrow.

Thank goodness for calm people.

I stop at the pizza place, head for Marijo's, where I find her sitting on her back porch, cigarette in hand, still smelling of the asparagus field, of the dirt of the research farm where her essential efforts keep farmers in the know about every pest, every blight or mold, every possible function and malfunction of an asparagus plant. Hers and John's work is a lifeblood to this crop that keeps Oceana County on the map. She leans against the shade, exhausted but deeply attentive in the way she can be, and her steady voice is careful, "How is she?"

Marijo and I are very different people: she's a warrior; I'm a placater—though we can switch roles in sudden storms. But she knows me deeply, and when I crack, she takes my hand. After a while we stand. We eat pizza and drink wine. She's as worried as I am, as deeply concerned, but too tired to be her fighting self. She decides to let the fields be, go with me to the ER in the morning. I am so grateful I tear up again. I could not appreciate her more.

Mercy Hospital in Muskegon, the ER, a tiny sterile room with a gurney and locked white cupboards, and we are an hour into an endurance test, and Mom is thirsty but they won't let her have fluids just in case she has to go into emergency surgery. I sit in a hard chair and bite my nails. Finally, from surgery, Dr. Leven sends orders to remove the cast first—he will come as soon as he can get away. Jackie, the nurse we have been assigned, brings John, a physician's assistant, into this room of hidden supplies. They examine the cast. Agreement—that sucker needs to come off.

For the second time into this troubling, not-yet-halfway year, I will see a cast removed from my mother's leg. This second troubling is what chews my nails to nubs. These two casts have everything to do with keeping things in place. But they haven't worked, have gone awry. Fact is, they may have solved the problem of broken bone, but each time, complications. And here's the poorest fact of all: I am a writer who makes meaning of stuff like casts that do not do their jobs. But I'm still struggling with this second-time-around metaphor. I thought I'd found meaning, figured it out, and decided. Now, to think it all through again, the role I have been cast in, the role she cast herself in, seems repetitious. Why is this happening? Because the first reset—get that bone in place, realign our relationship—worked only halfway. There was a too long delay in changing. Oh, I had changed my thinking—so I thought—but kept on behaving as I always did, delay in Detroit, and all the other demands of this literary life I believe is mine. Now we must break yet another cast to discover the unseen, unspoken infection.

Unlike the saw they used for the removal of the first cast, this one resembles a vacuum and looks remarkably like a small soldier at attention. Five of us and the soldier crowd the cubicle. They start the motor, and a high whir overruns our ears. I will myself not to faint—I am not good with blood. I expect blood. John steps right to it, applies the edge. The saw does not spin, but a slim line of separation reveals the cutting.

"How does it work?" I ask.

"Vibration. You could put this on your hand and you would get only a slight abrasion." Vibration. How many things in this world open under vibration. Earthquakes and fine china. Windows and sound. And also: anxiety, remorse, the guilty heart. You do not see the blade; there is none. The cut happens anyway.

I watch this second movie of the broken leg. Slow, knee to toe. Right side. She winces when he has to make the corner at the heel. He stops, asks her if she's okay—she nods. The left side. Knee to toe. The whine is a terrible insect, but there is no dust, and the seam down each side allows the leg to remain cradled. The cast is cracked open. Odor rises; the nurse gags. John stops the machine, gently shifts and wiggles the cast piece that should now be loose. He tries to lift; it won't give way. We hold our breaths.

Mom stares at us, "Well, what now?" Exactly. The question is not aimed at me, but I take it personally.

But it is John who answers. "I need the spreader." He leaves the room. We wait—no deep breaths. Jackie takes a package of gauze, opens the top, and pours air freshener over it—makes a little paper sign that says, "Do not use." Shrugs. Even with the air freshener, the smell makes us feel ill. She can see my mother is tiring. From some pocket on the machine, she pulls out a screwdriver and studies the cast. Then places its tip carefully into the top of the seams, and a quarter inch at a time, with slow care, she slides down the cut, loosening one part of the cast from the other. She finds where the two parts are connected. With that knowledge, she picks up the saw again, pushes start, and in slow motion, reinserts it into the already cut seam, putting light pressure on the stuck part. Mom gives a little jerk.

Jackie stops. "Did that hurt?"

My mom shakes her head. "It tickles." Now Mom seems interested and unafraid, watching. Now that she is not waiting—the room is full of people focused on her—she's enjoying this.

Gradually, with small pryings, Jackie loosens the cast's hold, and just as John returns with the spreader, Jackie angles the puzzle piece up. Mom let's out a small whimper. Marijo and I are touching her, trying to keep her or ourselves calm. John ends up using the spreader after all, one cut is stubborn, that spot right around the ankle, just below the bloom. I tell myself, this must be where the blood drains; this is where it would stick. Using both hands, they slowly lift and pull. Mom's shoulders tense, as do mine, and my fingers dig in. She turns, meets my eyes. My mother's eyes are afraid, a reflection of my own.

And then we are both looking at that leg, knowing what will be revealed, that story of what healing is left to her. A word comes to me. I *recognize* her leg. The varicose veins, the big ones like vines, the smaller ones tracing their spider tendrils, the shape of her calf, even with swelling at the ankle, all of it is the map of my childhood, her once powerful speed now broken. I know it. And also something else. Even if she couldn't speak the word, she would remember from her training: infection.

Memory rises, a way-back moment triggered by scent. The goose they kept in the barnyard, the large white gander who was fierce, and me wandering inside that fence to play with the cats, wandering toward the barn, and the goose gone territorial, and there in the light, the creature had exploded toward me, half flying, landing directly in front of me, pecking my knees and legs, nipping and honking and flapping against my small calves as I turned to run, screaming that kind of scream that is one long breath. She came. She came on those long legs already rivered with veins but long striding, the long fierce stride that I would eventually inherit. She came running from the garden, running strong, saddle shoes clomping in determination as fierce as the goose's. She kicked the goose, kicked it away as it hissed and honked—still pissed, and she pulled me into her arms, and she scolded me for screaming. We are *not to scream* about this; there will be *enough to scream about* in life: that *mean gander is not among them*. But she'd held me; I had forgotten that. She held me.

Then another memory, like a telescope extending into sections through our past, those legs again, once so young and unblemished, all the way back to her own escape to Chicago, that *running*, her own *leaving* her mother's house. Of course, she too was called home, to care for him, but that led to the nurses training, where she had finally found herself. The war ended, the boy she would marry came home, and they found each other. Or had they; she had walked into marriage slowly. When Dad asked her, she told him she had to think about it. She made him wait a week before she said yes, but then, she committed. When I first heard that tale, I thought it was about her being coy, playing hard to get; now I saw. It was that she knew she had legs, that she could walk away, legs to run on, and she had confidence in them. She was sure of my father, but of marriage? She knew it would change the map she had followed, the very shape of her running her life. Her purpose would shift, would be of rescue—her children, who would be nipped by geese and fall in the dust, the farm, that all-consuming god and gander—but not independence. In this bloom of memory, that revelation. Those legs, my legs. When it came to life, we were both runners.

The other thing we all see. The wounds. One fully open, revealing an interior—it comes to me—like a tomato slice. The other, like a squashed sweet cherry with the pit bursting forth. Both open. The cherry one is infected. The larger one, I realize, has no skin—whatever was left must have been taken up with the cast—and fresh flesh, swollen, exposes the bright tendon. The room is quiet as we study this revelation.

Jackie says, "Ulcerated." Ulcer. Abscess, pustule, boil—synonyms ratchet through my brain, but this word feels as accurate as light shone on a secret. This open flesh is ulcerated. Then Jackie does three tender things. She takes a pad of gauze and pours disinfectant on it, and gently lays one over each open wound, as if covering something private. She dampens small towels, soaps them up in the sink and begins to wash my mother's leg. Marijo and I see how it's done. We too glove up, pull chairs close—but it's a strange process, some skin releases in sheets like paper shards, and some flakes and pills like old wool. What's revealed shines as thin and fragile as Christmas tissue—I don't know if it should be revealed, if it should be opened to the air. It is delicate, this new skin.

When the doctor arrives, he is quick, he is efficient, he calls the wounds "cast sores" (a much less interesting term). "They'll heal—just takes a long time." He is more interested in what he can't see, in the bones under that skin. He pulls gloves on and puts his hands around the bones above her ankle. Here is another test. A soft shift.

He nods. "Still some movement. But there's soft bone in there. That's good," he assures, "that will be just fine for now." He gives orders for dressings, a new cast. A transition cast. A boot strong enough to hold the soft bone in place but light enough to keep the wounds healing. A boot that is a cast that can be removed at night, that might lead to some bearing of weight.

If she could have kept her independence, could have worn the boots I wear in my life, would she have said yes to our father, yes to us, this family, to five children, to the work of a farm, to kicking away a goose, to an eldest daughter who was more like what she had wanted to be, a person who left, not a runaway, but one who ran toward whatever shone, ran without caution—and got nipped. That was the cast that had festered. But now, a boot, a different kind of cast, one for transition.

The doctor shakes our hands. We thank him and he goes. I step out, bring Mom iced water, which she drinks deeply. Marijo slips away and returns with bundles of fresh asparagus for Jackie, John, and the others. Mom is so tired that if she speaks at all, she sounds drunk. I tell Marijo to leave and she does—she has fieldwork waiting for her. Full hard days ahead. As she leaves, she promises, "Mom, remember? McDonald's when you get home."

Mom lights up. "Fries?"

"And a cheeseburger." Marijo too is balancing love and work, better than I have.

I turn the lights down, sit in the near dark, holding Mom's hand, almost giddy with relief. There in the dark, another memory. The first time I ran, left her and all of them. My yes to myself; my no to her. The year I studied in England, the summer after. I came home, having attended University of Lancaster for ten months. She had thought I would get it out of my system, this thing about leaving, thought that I would come home and she would know me as I had once been, her oldest, difficult, overly dramatic daughter, but home for good.

I was not that person. Though I had missed my siblings badly, missed my father more deeply than I could say, truth be told, I hadn't missed her. I had done everything she would have said no to: I had smoked French Gauloises and more than a little hashish, demonstrated for an instructor who was fired for being a Communist, bought mod clothes with skirts so short they were indecent, drank dark Belgian beer (and Glenfiddich when I could get it), read Henry James, James Joyce, Doris Lessing, and Marx. I had worked in a pub, fell for a boy with an Irish accent, crossed the Irish Sea to see his war of Irish troubles—complete with assault rifles, strip searches, bombs, and tea service—climbed deep into the cave of O'Neill's ancient hill, and made love for the first time. I had traveled to my paternal family's ancestral home in the Netherlands. I had seen the windmill turn toward the Atlantic.

I could not come home.

I came home in body, of course. The year was over, and I had a degree to finish, that much I knew. But in spirit, I would never be home again, never again love or live on that farm, that land. She couldn't comprehend that. That cast had set. I left again in the fall of my senior year for college and did not come back until Christmas. We were both relieved.

The only way to break the cast was to find a way for us. "These boots are made for walking," the song said. The only way for me to walk was toward her—a person I was only beginning to know.

Jackie comes in to say goodbye; her shift is changing. I give Mom a toothpick, and after we have each gnawed one to a nub, we have a toothpick fight. She chuckles but then starts to weep. I remind her about Marijo's promise: McDonald's. Fries. It isn't much, but she settles. I return to her leg, washing again, and with each stroke, more dead skin peels away.

BITTER

Ideas rise and fall through the visits, and in the silence of sitting near her on the days I visit, I am coming to a new idea, a piece of fruit that I am not easy with tasting, the idea that change occurs not only in the mind but in the body, in the body and in its associated memories, its deep cellular memory, not only in the work of memory-meaning but in the process of physical action embedded in memory, in discovering that while trying to take care of Mom in her small room, in her aging body, I am also discovering things about my own memories, memories I thought I had right, thought were set.

"She hasn't been swallowing her pills." Lydia, the nurse, enters Mom's room at the Manor and announces this to me. I've already been through this with the day staff, but Lydia, part of the second shift, says it as though it is news. As though I can make my mother something different than what she is.

I nod. "Does she have pneumonia again?" My subtext: what? She can't swallow?

"No." Like I didn't hear her. "She won't swallow her pills." *Can't? Won't?* I don't ask. I nod again. "I'll try." I want to avoid another crisis. Marijo managed last week's bronchitis. This one's on me. But swallowing? Hard pill to swallow? The word play seems deliberate. And then, gosh, isn't swallowing a "life" skill, like you have to do it to eat? Like, it's part of survival? Like without it, you die?

Or is it the bitterness more than pills: all winter she has not been well. The new boot cast, though it can be removed at night, is cumbersome. Being bound to the wheelchair has made her incontinence worse, the lack of exercise has diminished muscle control even more, and that determined personality is being daily compromised by the encroaching dementia.

I stare out the window at brown lawn and barren trees. Evening, late winter. Dark comes on, extending a dusk that lingers each day longer. This evening, shadows sharp as knives, clear edged on the ice-crusted snow. The lawn of the medical care facility, right next door, is sprinkled with black licorice sticks, broken tree branches from last week's ice storm. They spell an ominous message. Under the birdfeeder, empty shells.

Swallowing is such a gift, that small winging in the throat, tiny contraction as you take in sustenance you love. That pleasure. And pain—a memory: we kids taking pills when we were fevered. Pills were like poison, like swallowing fire. She said to each of us, curled in those rumpled beds, "Get it to the back of the throat, and don't think about it. Wash it down." We would gag into the sheets. Now, she gags into her sheets. She who taught us all.

The aides gave up after the required second try. On her charts, it will say "refused." If she doesn't take these now, or at least the one final pain pill of the day, she will be in serious pain tonight, and that will keep her and everyone else in a different kind of pain along with her.

She can sip. She can take little sips of water through the straw. She loves cold water, always eager for the soothing quality in her mouth, down her dry throat. But only little sips. Little sip, little sip, and only if it's icy cold. As children, when we were asked to carry well water to the fields in plastic jugs, she would tell us to *let it run through the hose until it's so cold it hurts*. I stood there at the well, running the water over my hands until my fingers numbed. Of course, by the time we carried it all the way to some godforsaken field, it would have lost its delicious chill. She would spit out the tepid stuff. Like she now spits those pills.

In between her dosing, I log on to the Manor's on-again, off-again Wi-Fi to research swallowing. I try not to think about what it means if she can't swallow anymore. Sitting in that winter-tired room of my mother's, I learn swallowing has four stages. The oral preparatory phase is the part where you chew and form the bo-lus (great word!), that wad of food. Then comes the second phase, the oral transit phase, where you move the bolus to the back of the throat so you can swallow. The tongue elevates and rolls back, shift-ing the bolus backward. This would be the point where one gets that pill to the back of the throat quickly, so that it's in place for that tiny wave of epiglottal closure. That closure, part three, allows for food, or pills, to slide down; the contraction forces it to enter the pharyn-geal phase, where the swallowing actually occurs. The esophageal stage is when food finally passes through the esophagus into the stomach. Done.

I sit in her blue chair and swallow self-consciously, testing new knowledge, concentrating on the mechanics. I swallow compul-sively until my mouth goes dry; no bolus, no grit of burger or pie to chew and work with my tongue. An empty mouth makes her as-pirin even more bitter, the edges of pills feel like blades. No wonder it's hard.

When did we learn to swallow pills? We were children. Mumps, along with almost every other child in the school. I was ten, Patti four. Five of us in a month. Long before liquid aspirin, but I think she'd gotten baby aspirin. She taught us. Do it quickly, do it with cold water, tip our heads forward and slightly down so that the pill would float on the water to the back of the throat. We had cried—our throats swollen and aching. Then she had purchased ginger ale and given it to my siblings to make it easier. The fizz helped, but still, it was hard.

There was something else, something that had done the trick for the sickest.

And then she got sick too. An adult with mumps, a mother sicker than her children at a time when that new field of asparagus had to be planted, late spring, bitter. April with its frost-chilled winds. Her

will pulled her body, and she had taken me with her, the one of five
nearly better by then, out to the field to press down on the crowns
with my foot for the turning of the soil. She, running with chills
and fever and exhaustion, her face the size of a pumpkin, walked
ahead, bound to the crowns of asparagus by some cold-wind commitment beyond comprehension.

I had hated it, hated the planting that sent us both into those
biting fields, hated that I was the one who had the lightest case,
was even then most resilient, who needed to *step up and help out*,
hated most of all that I could not get her attention because the little girls, Marijo and Patti, were so much more sick than I was. I
was oldest, *didn't I know that, a big girl now*. I wanted to be smaller,
younger, sicker, wanted to be so sick that I could have ginger ale,
could have her hand on my forehead, could have her hold me, rock
me. I wanted my siblings to disappear, not to be dead but simply
gone. Just her and me and some deep-seated, egocentric sense that
she was mine alone, and I was hers. *Rescue* is the word that comes to
mind, that intimacy between the one who needs saving and the one
saving—that's what I wanted even when I knew already she could
not even rescue herself from this hard-work farm, her hard-work
life. Mumps with five kids. Planting asparagus in bitter April wind.
I had swallowed my own bitterness like a pill right there and then.
And kept it down.

Lydia brings the night pills. We wake Mom as gently as we can,
touching her shoulder, her cheek. "Mom, Mom, time to take the
pain meds."

She shakes her head. Actually, it's a deep shudder, shoulders
raised, forehead crumpled, more moving than she's done all day.
She's deep into the circus of sleep. She is asked to be the swallower
of a fiery sword, and if she does not perform for this waking circus
of aides and nurses, she will be miserable, as will everyone else in
this circus.

I palm the three pills.

The big Motrin is the hardest. Because Mom's spine is now
shaped like a stem weighted by a too heavy blossom past its prime,

the esophagus collapses into a position that, even if she could get to the oral transit stage, it's a challenge to get to the pharyngeal phase, where food, pills, even saliva actually goes down. She ends up dissolving pills in her mouth. Bitter clouds. She gags again and again, spits it all up. I adjust her body position, trying to get her to sit up straighter, trying to straighten the stem.

This is harrowing. This is about throat work when it's confused. This is about that almost mechanical thing that happens in the complex fleshy apparatus of the throat, which is not a flower, has none of the openness of the flower's throat. How to swallow. How to swallow a sword that is a pill that is bitterness. She's stuck. It's called dysphagia. Swallowing disorders, one of the signs in old age that things are going awry.

She is hurt by my insistence.

Then it comes back, another shard of memory, about those mumps. I had nearly forgotten. I ask Lydia to bring it, the only thing I can think of, what I will know about my mother to the last moment, that love of sweetness. By the time Lydia does, it's nearly dark. I bury the pill in that softened ice cream, ask Mom to sit up as straight as she can in order to open her throat. I scoop an inch. Enough? I lift the spoon to Mom's mouth, tuck it in. She sucks down the ice cream and spits out the pill. I've let bitterness dissolve and ruined the sweetness.

"Mom, Mom, just get this to the back of your throat. Let the ice cream melt a little, then just swallow. Remember how you used to tell us?" Just get to the pharyngeal phase, Mom. The phase where the little epiglottis flips down, the breathing for half a second stops, and the contractions that mark the actual swallow begin. Another scoop, bigger, the pill inserted. "Just swallow," I coach. *Your words, Mom*, like other lessons, like *stand up straight*, like *breathe deep*. Like *bring water so cold it hurts your teeth*.

Tears stream down her face. And then she swallows. Down.

I thrust another pill into the ice cream, get her to lift her head, straighten the esophagus, tip her chin, and after another struggle, she gets that one down. I praise her as I would a child. "That's so good, Mom. You did it."

She gives me a version of the stink eye she reserves for our worst offenses, that telepathic *you just wait.* "Waste of good ice cream," she mutters.

The third pill is a stool softener. I throw it in the trash. She sees me do it. Nods, seriously pleased about this breach of protocol. When Lydia enters with a fresh glass of ice water, the question large on her anxious face, I say with enthusiasm, "She took them all."

"She's not cheeking?" Lydia asks. Mom has been known to cheek her pills. Mom sticks out her tongue, not merely to reveal to Lydia that her mouth is clear. Lydia approves; her night will be easier. Mom settles back and I scoop another spoonful, just plain sweetness. This time it's easy; this time it goes down with pleasure. I could crow. "That was a real swallow."

"Where?" she asks, looking at the window. The bird feeder hangs, waiting to be filled.

"Long gone now," I say. Only sweetness is left. Only some quiet rest for the body, a swallow now arching over the bitter fields of the past. Her right hand, the one so compromised by arthritis, lifts and makes a little motion, like a wing tipping, like a bird turning in flight.

BIRD DOG VISITS

Early fall, months-of-the-same later, my sister-in-law Jackie and
my niece Kristin come to visit Mom at the Manor. They bring the
dog, the great hunter. They lead him into my mother's room, the
ticked and liver-spotted pointer, Buck, now in his ninth year, broad-
chested, restless with the diet they have put him on because they
are preparing for the pheasant hunting in late November. He is
overweight and summer lazy. They need him hungry and eager.
They bring him to visit to keep him moving, to get him used to
commands again, used to new people and new situations because
he will need to hunt hard in immense grasslands with strange men.
He is an aristocrat, a dignified animal, submitting but always with
deliberateness: he does this as a gift, not as obeisance. But here, in
room 116, in the midst of chatter and news, he meets his match.

He stops at the door, head rising to the scent, and then enters
quietly as though analyzing a current, tracking yes, a new creature.
He lowers his head to the carpet, trailing an enormous bird he has
never before encountered. He sniffs the stained floor with intense
interest, stilling in certain spots for long periods of time, then moving on slowly, nose pulsing like a heart. There's power here, even
he knows that, and then his nose leads him to Mom's wheelchair,
and he sniffs quietly every inch of the wheel, round and round both
of those wheels, up to the arms of the chair, around the back, each
arm, its entire length, his nose trembling with whatever epic history the scents of her age give to him. Some experts say that, for

dogs, scent is like a love story in a movie, and perhaps it is so in that room, for once he knows the source, he does not take his eyes from my mother, her throne of odor, he of the great snout, of the sure run through those tall grasses of the Dakotas, Montana, Wyoming, fields where the pheasants, the kingly birds, hide everywhere, hard to find without a good dog, no, a great dog with a great nose, though this dog's years were past seventy. The hunters said he had the softest mouth of all, and now this great dog with his saddle markings like a maroon cape wants nothing more than to rest his head on my mother's lap, my mother's hand on his brow, his nose shivering with joy at the accidental and terrible scent of her aging, her incontinence, his adoration rising like a wonder. The only sound that he makes for the entire hour rises when they leash him to leave, and he lets out a long sigh, and then a small whine, so unlike him. He is scolded, and he raises his head and views everyone in the room with disappointment, and he leans up and licks my mother's hand and turns to leave and does not look back at the bird that for those moments, the great white-plumed bird, defined his life.

But for me, this small moment, as I watch it, is a final moment of reckoning. There is something in the air, and it's not just an odor, not running out of money, not trying to learn what makes a good daughter, and not just that the aides can't keep up with her lack of hygiene, can't always get her to take her meds. There is a cloud gathering in that room, and it's not just the result of incontinence. It's a scent; it's been there for a while, but now it has definition.

The scent is neglect.

FLOWERS: A SERIES

1. STALE MUMS

Therese, the director at the Manor, is a friendly woman with a good heart who knows the aging process, knows the work of running a home for the aged, knows our family, and most important, knows Mom. She sits behind her office desk piled with stacks of forms and a vase of long-past-prime mums. We are having a talk. About Mom. What we both know. Since Mom broke her leg, and all the complications and months of healing, she's needed more attention in every way, from hair washing to extra therapy. Therese also knows the numbers; the cost of Mom's care has increased. Of course it has. We're at the end of her funds. I explain this to Therese, trying not to sound like I'm whining, trying not to sound like I'm making excuses, trying to discover what she can offer. Therese nods with compassion. The screen behind her blinks. A half-eaten sandwich on the laden desk wafts a dry-bread scent.

I tell her we may attempt to sell Mom's house, but it might take a while to find someone who wants a house that remote. Therese sighs. She swivels in her big desk chair, studies the screen, swivels back. "Your mother is at the highest level of care we can give her."

"I'm grateful for the extra attention."

"Our aides spend more time with your mom than with anyone else right now."

"I can see that, the changing, even the boot cast is heavy..." I trail off.

She smiles wanly and continues, "You can see how frail she is now, how much therapy, specialized care . . ." Her turn to trail off.

"Could Mom go to a semiprivate?" She'd hate that but it might extend her time.

"I wish but no."

She's not willing to negotiate? My heart races, and I feel my voice getting ready for challenge. As if reading my objection, she says, "Her dignity and their privacy, both for your mom in her state, and for the others she shares with."

Okay. I can see that. But there must be a path through this. Really.

She says it gently, says it with quiet integrity. Still, the words shock me. "It's time." The screen blinks softly, the sandwich sends up its old scent, the mums look teary-eyed.

What she is saying aloud and into the air at last: our mother needs more care than they can give her. Even if we could afford it, in the silence of Therese's office, I hear the answer at last: the Manor is no longer the place for that care. And if the Manor is not the place, then . . . where?

The scent of the dying mums is almost overwhelming. I can't see my way forward. Or rather, the paths I can see forward are not the ones I want for my life or Marijo's. And that's it, isn't it? That's who I am. That is still, after all this time, after all these slow-blooming awarenesses I have been given through her care, this is still who I am.

I thank her and leave the office, the mums and sandwich and the woman who tells the truth, and walk down the long hall. I go to Mom, kiss her on the cheek, and feel like Judas or Peter or one of the other great betrayers of history—they are all standing behind me, building up layers of glee that another has joined the ranks.

2. TRUMPET VINE

In what happened to us lies a pattern, blurred and varied, that upends many families among boomers, a microcosm of the cultural macrocosm. If you're lucky, as we were, it starts with a family meet-

ing, and it's friendly—there may be beer. Raise a Stella Artois to
that. We sisters gather—me, Marijo, and Pat, it's we who must take
the first step. We stand on the deck of Mom's empty river house,
staring at the river below, that horseshoe shape that swirls toward
us and away, as though the river were deciding. Behind us, shadows
cast by a trumpet vine, the orange horn-shaped blossoms faded on
the wind. They are, of course, silent.

We are drinking beer for the worst of reasons—we don't know
what to do.

Like so many betrayals, this one was well intentioned. This time,
it's about trust. Legal and otherwise. All those decades ago when my
parents placed their assets in a family trust, they looked proactive.
That trust was to be used for their care when they were too old to
take care of themselves. Or if one died, the money was to be applied
to the other's care. So, they continued to live comfortably, quietly
setting aside those CDs, creating that savings from their pensions,
social security, plain frugality. We adult children are authentically
grateful they'd had that much money, that they had, in fact, antici-
pated many things, and the money had, with Marijo's careful bud-
geting and some help from the brothers, stretched as far as it had,
nearly five years. And it should have been enough; except when we
lost Dad, we didn't do what they had expected but had never said
they wanted. We didn't take Mom on, didn't take her in; we talked
her into, *ahem*, the Manor. So yeah, *all taken care of*. She was taken
care of at great expense by other people. That was the trust we had
marred until the means for the betrayal was spent. Now she needs a
nursing home, a full-scale medical care facility, at full pay upward
of ten thousand dollars a month—a staggering amount.

We've brought that six-pack of Stella only to realize that not
one of us has an opener, and the house is empty—mocking us. Finally, Marijo mangles two caps together and pops them off, spilling
a froth of yeasty flowers wetly onto the deck. Wasted beer. We hate
that.

It's complicated further: the final understanding that now surfaces. The oversight. Dad and Mom had wanted us to have something, but they hadn't considered what would happen if all the

money in the trust were liquidated for one person's care. They hadn't imagined it going to zero. Now, all that's left is the house. Which is how Marijo and Pat and I find ourselves leaning on the deck rail, staring at the river, talking about the trust.

Can anyone read that thing?

Is it really a trust if it doesn't protect anything?

We didn't understand that.

They didn't understand that.

This last one hurts. We'd been naive but so had they. If we had studied it, realized, and diplomatically objected, would they have listened? Hard to say. And what would we say anyway? We drink our Stellas. We stand in the shadows, watching the river run its course around the horseshoe peninsula. In dusk-dredged light, we slowly see what has been lurking under all this since Dad died. This final awareness, ping-ponging among us. By the time we open the second round of Stellas, the beery shadows under our shoes are darkening into the redwood deck.

Everything else is gone.

The trumpet vine rustles in an upcurrent breeze. I turn to study it, leaning back on the deck rail. I remember the vine was transplanted from our mother's mother's little house in Elbridge. The vine wobbles in the wind, tentative on its trellis. We all remember Grandma Julia standing on the porch of her little house and her trumpet vine winding up, wrapping itself around the posts and draping off the roof as if crowning her in sunset. Mom loved that plant, brought the cutting with her to this house when it was new to them. Decades later, this is what's left. A legacy shrub, a vine that clings thickly to a rickety trellis, tenacious but tired.

As if reading my thoughts, Marijo finally asks it, *Is this the legacy?* And then the beer is gone and the dark has come on, and the river horseshoes its way beyond us and through the distant farms.

3. WHITE TULIPS

I park on an angle as directed by the street signs. Multiple directions, contradictory timelines.

Step one: Pull out the box from the back seat of the car.

Step two: Stand at the edge of the street and try not to run away. Or not run back to the Manor and tell Mom we will take her home, care for her as an elder in her own home.

Step three: Cross the street, enter the plain brown building.

Step four: Meet the lawyer. Shake his hand.

The lawyer has a remarkable, strangely animated, utterly distracting handlebar mustache, but he is smart, no-nonsense, and has experience with this kind of situation. He settles into a chair on one side of the long dark conference table decorated by some artificial tulips so white they are baptismal. I settle the box of Mom's papers on the other side and begin removing documents just so that he doesn't think I am a complete idiot.

My first question, "Is this legal?"

It may be. Depends on how the trust was written.

"It's twenty pages."

A trust is not your friend.

"Can we amend this thing?"

Perhaps, or close the trust.

"Can you clarify?"

I'll have to review.

"In the meantime?"

Spend down her accounts to under two thousand dollars.

Pay all the bills, keep receipts.

Pay the last of the funeral expenses.

Close other accounts and be prepared to prove it.

No gifts to yourselves. Not a cent.

Get a fair market value on the house.

Get all records in good order.

I make the list as though I did this every day.

"How much will it cost?" He tells me. I swallow. I ask how long the process takes, calculating hours.

Don't count on anything, but if we're lucky, a few months.

If we're lucky? I feel like an idiot.

In the end, he has the documents he needs. He knows what he is doing. I write the first check. I don't ask what he can't answer: is this the right thing for my mother? I leave the room of fake tulips and carry the box out to the car to discover I was illegally parked all along.

4. PEONY

Now we know. If Mom were to have no more than two thousand dollars in assets, she could apply for Medicaid. But to do that she can't have access to a trust, even a trust that contains only an empty house, which yes, we could sell, which would give her about a year of care at the cost of a full-scale medical care facility. Then we'd be back here where we started—and no house. Marijo and I have each explained these finances to her, together and separately, more than once. We helped her follow the conversation, gave her a chance to be part of the conversation, and more importantly, to be part of the decision. Finally, she asked, "Can we talk to the boys." She wants to consult her sons.

We gather, four of the five siblings, at the Manor's gazebo just after the solstice—that marking of long days after the end of asparagus season, after summer heats up, as the earth begins to tip away again. Pat's in Colorado but has agreed to whatever we decide. We don't know if the Medicaid option is salvation or if it's even possible, because we're still waiting for the lawyer's review. But the real question: if the lawyer says it is possible, should we actually apply? Marijo and I have lost sleep about this, and the phone line to Pat in Colorado has been tearful.

It is a time of summer flowers. I can scent the blooms on the wind, even there.

In the gazebo, in the presence of my brothers, Marijo and I repeat again to Mom what we have learned. If we don't sell the house, if we want to save it, there is only one option: to petition the courts to close the trust (to protect her last asset, the house) so she can apply for Medicaid. We don't know if it's legally possible, but if it is, do we have her blessing?

Marijo chimes in, explaining details I have missed. Marijo is good at this, the explaining part, but she projects her voice at Mom in a way that Mom hears perfectly but resents. We never understand this, Mom's unpredictable abruptness with Marijo. Mom turns, stares at the garden. For a moment, her chin lifts and I see her old defiance and I expect her voice to shrill up and it makes me so happy I could cry—not because she'll scold us all, not because she'll defy the idea, but because it's a flash of spirit, a slice of who she was, that anger and resilience, thrusting that chin. She does not speak; her lips shape a thin line sharp as a knife. We wait through a silence so long I have to look out over the garden to see what she sees. There, peonies waffle in wind, a wash of pink and pale rose and white, another of the blossoms of our childhoods, the blooms she grew along the edge of the yard on the clay field, the ones from which she insisted we pick off the rose chafers. I loved peonies, the spice and faded citrus scent, but hated those hard-armored bugs. And I remember the result. Every peony we purged of chafers got taken to the church. They weren't for us. She cut bouquets for June's Sunday masses, for the altars to be graced with the heavy pink and white, the scent of summer. I straighten my shoulders. There, under the roof of the gazebo, a scent to love embedded with memory, a decision to loathe embodying the future.

Then, as she looks toward the peony light, she says a thing so familiar, so practiced, so utterly her that I don't know why I didn't expect it, didn't predict it.

She says, "I'll think about it."

This is the line she and Dad used to ward off any big decision until no decision was possible. This was the rehearsed and polite response they had agreed to say to anyone trying to sell them anything they didn't want or couldn't afford. If they wanted to delay saying no, or any confrontation, even hurting someone's feelings, this was how they did it. In any case, *I'll think about it* had nothing to do with thought. *I'll think about it* meant *not on your life*. I want to spit.

Again, the scent. Maybe she is saying this because she does not fully understand. Or does not remember what we've said. The cognitive issues of dementia? Or is she really putting us off, confused but still cunning?

I look to my brothers. They've done what they could. No one faults them. Only now are they beginning to understand the frustration we sisters have felt about the reverence my mother puts in their opinions. Since they haven't offered any, my mother will *think about it.*

This meeting is over. We deliver Mom to her room and walk together in silence down the long hall, but as we say our goodbyes in the foyer, my brothers, who I think now do at last have a real sense of what this means, both say the same thing: *Go ahead. If there's a way, petition the court.* It's all Marijo and I need to hear. I didn't expect it, but I feel so grateful I tear up.

5. WHITE TULIPS AGAIN

Back at the lawyer's dark and shining conference table, I'm biting my nails, waiting for his review. The silk tulips look on, dustier and more determined than ever. He enters, handlebar mustache freshly waxed. He sighs. *Your family's trust is perplexing.*

Speak of the obvious: he's the third lawyer to look at it.

But there's a loophole…

A loophole? Lordy, how does that work?

A clause. Two doctors must declare your mother unable to care for herself. It's called a declaration of incompetence.

A clause that hurts my ears.

Once established, it means we can petition the courts to close the trust. Deny your mother access.

I don't stop to think; I don't think about the end point—a court date. I ask for details, how to get these letters, which doctors, the cost. I leave the lawyer's office with my cuticles bleeding, and finally in the car, I ask myself: if I were her, is this what I would want? I know the answer already. This is how we care for her body, this is how we starve our souls.

6. LILACS

My brother Rick and Jackie's kitchen. Pat home from Colorado
to see Mom, to relieve Marijo, and to be with us. Chips and salsa,
cheese layered with homemade venison, and some rare jerky made
from wild game— delicious but we don't much taste it. We are trying to talk. The stakes, not necessarily in order: petition the court,
declare her incompetent, close the trust, save the house, apply for
Medicaid, leave the Manor, move to the full-scale medical care facility right next door. Once everything is in place, it's dominoes, right?

But we are having trouble with this. There's a ghost in the room,
a ghost that has always been there but one about which we have
not much spoken. Yes, we are grappling with legality, our Mom's
resistance, our own guilt. But it is my father's ghost whose presence plays in our midst and plays with our minds. We all know that
Dad was a deeply conservative man who generally distrusted government programs, who would have rolled over in his grave at our
accepting what he would perceive of as *entitlements*. Even for Mom.
What it means. If we follow what we know were his wishes, his belief that you never take anything from the government, that you
take care of your own, then we abandon the plan, sell the house,
and when the money is gone, we face this question all over again.
I've tried to anticipate what would happen, the cost out of our own
pockets. In that case, we'd have to look for another place, a cheaper
place, a place where her care might be compromised at a time when
it's clear she needs more care. A place farther away from the core
of family, particularly from Marijo, who is always the point person closest to Mom. Or we go back to plan A, quit our jobs, take care
of her at home. Could we even manage that with her dependencies
now? The question hangs there again, once more alive.

This is hard, this plan that could help her, provide for her, could
save a small familial home, but it's not how we have been taught,
not how it was supposed to go, and not how Dad would have wanted
it to go.

This was the part I couldn't anticipate, that I would begin to feel less obligation and more real concern because of memory. Memory has been, for lack of a better description, blooming. With every trip home, every week, something arrives, rising up from every field and orchard I pass on the blue highways of that county, memory given off even from the flowers—all of them bring alive a past I had walled off. Does it change me, change the circumstances I feel trapped in, now that I remember?

But what of these other dear ones? In that family meeting, I see Marijo holding herself in. Marijo too understands the nuances and is trying not to be angry. Marijo's heart hurts so bad from all the repressed feelings that she can barely lift her head. She's holding on to the edge of the counter so she won't walk out. For her, this is even more fraught. I was in graduate school when she gave up her baby boy, and though long past, I will not forget the pain she felt when Dad had cried in shame after she told him she was pregnant. Marijo with her two-toned eyes and super sensitive nature feels this more deeply than my sturdy, no-nonsense brothers. Beyond my slow insights, Marijo's loss has deepened and she feels an even greater complexity, a more fraught psychic energy—Dad's will, our lives, what we want set against what we were taught. Dad's pride still holds sway, years after his death, and his perspective permeates the house, right down to the venison.

It happens again, right there at the kitchen island, memory slips in, a childhood spring when Marijo and Pat were very small and I was left in charge of them, and they were supposed to be playing in a tiny building we called the playhouse, a former chicken coop. But instead of playing there, corralled, Marijo and Patti hid under the lilac bushes, those laden purple arches, in the shallow troughs the dogs had dug to cool themselves. There, where the swollen bloom wafted with such weight we were nearly drugged with it, they had gathered dirt like iron to magnets. I went to Mom, tattling that they were hiding, that it wasn't my fault they were dirty. She came from the house, and I thought she would spank them, but instead, she shrugged, showed us all how to pick a single blossom from a frond of lilac and to suck the end, the sweetness, a tiny burst on the tongue, the smallest drop of nectar. She stood with her three daughters, two so small they may not have this memory. She stood briefly in the scent, teaching us the sweetness of lilacs, bees humming among the clouds of blossoms, a richness I had forgotten. I want that sweetness now, for her, for her middle daughter leaning on the counter. I don't know what to say to Marijo, to remind her of these lost pleasures. I don't know if there is ever comfort. I see Mom now, more every day, in these scented, lit-up memories that return from a past like kindling, broken and flammable: a mother who loved sweetness but who was so afraid of shame that she lost her kindness and wouldn't stand up to our father for the sake of her daughter. Or maybe she was just so beyond it all. This part, this part is the center for Marijo.

Besides Marijo, there had been another child under the lilacs. She has grown up too. There in that warm kitchen, Pat steps up. Pat has something to say. Pat makes a statement: "We want her safe—that's always been the goal, hasn't it? Medicaid will keep her safe. That gives Mom the means for good care, where they know what they are doing and they will provide the right services."

Pat takes a breath. She says aloud what Dad had missed all along. "It allows us to keep our jobs, pay our taxes, be productive members of society. That's what it's for. So we don't all become destitute in the process. You know what I mean?"

Pat rarely takes the light, tends toward the role of astute observer, but in this moment, she is doing bright thinking for us. This idea that allows us to be constructive citizens—a rational thought, a practical thought that lowers the emotional tenor in that hunt-scented room. How has my sister stated this so clearly? Look at the facts she asks: as workers, as taxpaying members of the nation, we are already putting in for this program called Medicaid. We are working, meeting a citizen's obligations, and so isn't this how we manage to keep on doing so? Her clarity cuts through my guilt-ridden *maybe-this maybe-that what-ifs*. And before the end of the night, we agree to go forward. The review, application, legal petition, court date, though this is where we all reach for the sliced meat sweating on the plate because this makes us feel so empty we have to fill the spaces. My father's ghost quietly leaves the room.

7. NIGHT BLOSSOMS

Lunch with Mom in the library at the Manor. Leftovers from supper, my David's richly smoked asparagus soup. But the plastic container is awkward, so she can't spoon it herself. I lift a dollop to her mouth, and she opens her mouth like a bird and makes a little hum in her throat.

Tomorrow, I will contact her doctor for the first letter.

I lift another spoonful. She opens and I slip it in.

The second doctor will be the bone doctor who reset her leg. He knows the truth about her walking. It isn't happening.

"Smoky. Very good." She nods. I have told her again all about the lawyer, about what Therese has said, what her sons and daughters plan to do. I tell her that if the court closes the trust, she will be legally in poverty. And that means she may be eligible for Medicaid, and if that goes okay, we will move her to the medical care facility, where she can get better therapy. The court date is set. The pieces are falling into place.

Each time, it abandons her. For so long, telling her everything seemed like the right practice, to repeat honestly the progress, the situation, how we have come to this. But now, each time she shakes her head, says no but quietly, as though she were whispering a wish. Then she forgets.

I dip and lift, and I wonder what kindness is.

A memory traces its way into that room of books. Once, when I was suffering a bout of childhood insomnia, when I was pacing the house in darkness, Mom woke and walked me out of doors into the night, through our cherry orchard full of moonlit and blossoming trees, up a hillside filled with that light. I was perhaps twelve, had some wounds by then, a boy had hurt me, there had been deaths in the family.

When I asked her why we were doing this, going outside, she said sharply, as if I were asking a stupid question, "To see the blossoms." So, we walked through that eerie light reflected on uncountable blossoms until I was calm enough to sleep. We walked through the heart of the orchard and stood among the silent trees in light that seemed tangible, and in the end, was comforting for simply being luminous—we knew it was beautiful even if there were no words, even if it didn't change a thing, the brush with beauty was somehow sweet comfort. I see now what I didn't see then: she too was awake, perhaps struggling. She needed to walk off worry, walk off some sorrow I did not have the empathy to imagine, to walk out a frustration that simmered, capped, under everything. She wanted a moment in the moonlight of the orchard, and she was willing to take me, awake too, with her.

We had lost that. It means there had once been something there, between us.

I hold the spoon. She opens her mouth like a child.

What I don't tell her is that I wish I could talk to her, really talk to her. I want to explain not just the circumstances of our situation over and over but how these memories now climb up and throw their light into jeweled air without order, how each one shows a different facet that I can't always read, don't know how to sharpen to clarity, and most of all I want to tell her how the word *incompetence* hurts, how I wake at night with it now, how I turn it around, point it toward myself and wonder about the rough edges in its syllables, how I walk alone with it. I want to know if she will forgive my incompetence: my trying to know her, but so poorly, as if I were using inadequate tools on purpose. Still, and this is where I pause to study her face among the books and from inside the small knowledge I gain with every memory, with every trip home. I decide this at last. I will never again tell her the circumstances of these decisions we are making for her. I will not explain again, repeat and repeat and expect her to understand or hope she will remember. I will not expect her to walk with me into this loss. I will hold it for her. It is the only kindness I can offer in return.

I slip in the spoon. She nods, savors the soup. I keep lifting, staying with the rhythm of soup. She opens and swallows. She murmurs something like words every time. But they are not words. If I made them up, what would I they be? *Go ahead, Anne, walk in the moonlight, study the blossoms in the dark orchard, suck the sweetness from the lilacs. But don't forget the rose chaffers on the peonies; you have to pick them off before we can take them to church—otherwise they fall on the altar.*

The soup's gone.

She studies the library shelves. "A lotta books," out of nowhere.

I ask her if she can still read large print.

"Of course." As if I were stupid. I know that she can't read my new book because the font is too small. Perhaps just as well—too much about her. But if she could . . . would she understand that trying to understand our relationship is one of the shaping forces of my life? That trying to understand why we did not easily walk together in the light as well as the dark, which is all she wanted, is still shaping me?

I sit, holding the empty spoon. Why did I run away? Why did I leave her? Why didn't I try harder to see through her anger, her pain, her loneliness standing in that blooming orchard? Because she was shrill and nothing was ever right? Because she struck me once? Because I became afraid of her? She haunts me, this mother who is now pursing her lips like a kiss.

There is a book on the lamp table. *Why We Suffer.* Large enough print? I hand her the book, and she opens it, and sure enough, as the quiet of postlunch settles, she reads slowly aloud, all the Christian reasons for why we suffer: to be closer to God, to purify ourselves, to understand the immensity of God's plan . . . She reads aloud without comprehending, and I watch as she reads the words one by one, rotely, that tell me why we suffer. None of them suit. None of them fit. But her reading aloud to me, her voice slowly working out the ancient process of sentences, there is some sacred nourishment in that, some scent of peony and lilacs and moonlight.

QUARTER WINDOWS

Mason County Courthouse in Ludington, a brick, four-story, modified American Romanesque (is there such a thing?) structure with all the variegated stone stripes now painted, appears as a solid red instead of the festive look pseudo-European buildings take on. It sits squat, with a pointy cupola, forbidding except for that tower pointing to some unseen justice in the firmament. David and I walk up the steps and enter the glass doors and tread the grand hallway, and there at the far end, the unassuming sign that says "Probate and Family Court." Three unmatched straight-backed wooden chairs stand under the sign, and I drop my purse in one and promptly start to pace. David settles easily in another, noting aloud the oak staircase, fine carved railings, and down a wide hall, another high-ceilinged room, where a 1961 map of Ludington, yellowed and huge, hangs in prominence. I stare at these things like I have no idea where I am. I turn, walk in another direction. David, watching me with concern, and without saying a word, let's me know I should get a handle on this anxiety I'm mainlining straight from my mother's spirit, the ever-present ghost that remains alive in me. His quiet says, *Here is where you are.* That is all he can say when I get like this. I slow, settle, try to observe with him the what and where of this time, to note the old polished details, to calm my heart, hoping I'll be able to think clearly when I'm asked questions. But then I start to walk again, though I do stay nearer his calm. I slow.

Gradually we gather, we four siblings who can attend this legal venture—Pat in Colorado has already signed paperwork. First, my brother Rick limps in, his gaunt face reminding me more every day of my father's father, the hooked nose, the piercing eyes of our Dutch grandfather. Rick's battered his knee in the middle of demanding fieldwork, and he wants to go on some great hunt somewhere in Canada but doesn't know if his knee will bear it because, as he says, "It's a young man's hunt."

The lawyer, Ray of the handlebar mustache, arrives next, today dressed in a sports jacket. He's in efficiency mode, explains what will happen, this thing we are about to do, and he leaves to speak with the court officers. Marijo arrives with a warm smile, her face a mix of reserve and canny watchfulness, and greets both Rick and me, and for a while we all admire the grand hallway rising to hold the county's legal service, and as we stand there, a workman balances his way down the stairs and through the hall carrying one part of a palladium circle window, a large window shaped like a quarter of a pie, solid wood framing nice glass. As he passes, Marijo asks what he intends to do with the old window.

"You want it?" he asks.

"Maybe," she says. "You got its mate?"

He does, of course. Three more, the whole set. Four quarters of a grand glass circle. Then he says, "They're by the dumpster—take what you want." She gets directions. She is in true form, charming and interactive, scarfing those four quarter circles even in the midst of this other story. The metaphor rises. My four siblings, the quarter windows of this decision.

Marijo identifies Tom's heavy steps on the stairs, just on time. His solid being signified with a careful nod and upright stance laced with skepticism. Our lawyer returns and leads us to a windowless basement room. It's the family courtroom and perhaps the smallest courtroom in the world. Five chairs at the back of a room that is the size of a large bedroom. School desks form the dividing rail between the judge's bench and the rest of us.

We say, "Well, look at that," about the school desks. Our lawyer lifts one lid to reveal an empty interior. Still, if there were children involved, this setting might be familiar, comfortable. To me, a kiddy courtroom for putting your elder in medical care seems beyond irony to the surreal.

Then the judge enters, tells us we may sit. "Identify yourselves please."

We do. Ray presents the case, explains the details of our mother's estate and state, that she can no longer care for herself, but that she cannot apply for government funds until her trust is closed. He explains how the trust was written, the clause that allows for this. He produces the doctors' letters. He produces other documentation.

Marijo and I have shared power of attorney, but because I'm the one who initiated the petition, the judge asks me to take the stand. I step forward, take the oath. Tell the truth. I do swear. To tell the truth. The judge tells me to have a seat. I take the stand as witness, the first step of the betrayal of this woman I am coming to understand in a way I had not expected.

He begins, "Where does your mother live?" The judge doesn't even look at the papers.

"Cherry Blossom Manor, a home for the aged. In Hart."

"When and of what did your father die?"

"June 14, 2010, of angiodysplasia of the colon, which led to heart failure."

"How long has she been in Cherry Blossom Manor?"

"After a year in and out of care, she has now been there for three years."

"What is her physical state?"

The questions are easy. The questions are hard. I sigh, feel the pressure mount in my eyes, ask myself for the millionth time if there is any other way this could be done, if there is any other approach. It is, clearly, too late.

"She's confined to a wheelchair." She's also incontinent, can barely see, and is in dementia. Do I need to say that?

"Can she care for herself on her own?"

"No." Before I can think how to expand, he asks the next question.

"What are the changes she is experiencing?"

"She can't walk. She can't drive. She can't pay her bills." She can't get to the bathroom, she can barely dress herself, barely use the phone, she doesn't see well. She is as kind to us as she has ever been, and she is so happy to see us when we come that it is like a light shining directly from heaven, but she can rarely extend a conversation. She can't scold us anymore.

"Does she have any remaining fluid assets?"

"No." She has an empty house. It is not considered fluid.

"Can she live as she did in 1989?" The year the trust was written.

"No."

"No further questions." Does he bang a gavel? I don't think so. I think he just says it. But there was something gavel-like in that *no further questions*. Something done. I have answered all the questions. I'm so startled, I sit for a few seconds too long, staring at him. Doesn't he know how much she hates what is happening to her, this going on alone in a home that is not her own, and how much we hate what we are doing. Or how much I feel like there must be another way. I want to speak, tell him every detail, say I am sorry it has all come to this. Ask forgiveness as if he were a priest and not a judge.

The judge flips pages on the desk, then announces that he sees no reason not to accept this petition. He signs papers, hands them to Ray to file. We rise as one, thank him, and he leaves the court room with us. Twenty minutes start to finish. It comes to me with no small shock: *the judge does this every day*. We are not the rare case; he's seen this a hundred times. He's heard a thousand reasons to evoke this process. Make people legally incompetent and, thus, eligible for governmental services. He understands exactly why we have come and how this is to be done.

We return to the light of the grand hall, shuffling as though waiting for more where there is nothing more. But then we agree to a beer at the Grand, one of the divey-est bars in Ludington. David holds my hand all the way to the car. We drive a few blocks. We stumble into the old bar like we have already been drinking, all slow and clumsy. Or maybe it seems that way only to me.

When Marijo joins us, she has already picked up the windows from the dumpster, stashed them in her car. We sit quietly, each with our thoughts. No one is happy: Rick is staring out a window, Tom into his beer, I'm tearing up damp napkins, Marijo is looking from one to another.

Tom finally asks Marijo, "Whatcha gonna do with those windows?"

She's thoughtful. "Make something new. Maybe one of those floating platforms you can hang over tables, you know?" She's already got something in mind. I see it, how you could place seasonal things so shadows would fall over a table or counter. Look up, see it from the underside, each different.

I say, "Maybe you could make a coffee table." No one picks up on that. "Or you could just use them as windows." They nod. Yes, you could use them as windows, look through each quarter, and each would give a different view, wouldn't they—with some overlap. Each of my siblings with our different views of our mother. We each got some portion of a truth we think we hold in total. Each one of us has a different relationship with that whole, with Mom. Rick and Tom were her beloved boys, who had worked with Dad and made good on the farm: Tom, the talkative, diplomatic one; Rick, the quieter, driven one. Both had escaped the worst of Mom's temper. They understood imperfectly the complexity of we three sisters' relationship with Mom. They could not touch it because she revered them. Marijo, the daughter who always felt like the black sheep lost in the flock, who could not escape their judgement but who built a good life, overcoming it all. Pat, the youngest, who escaped on her childhood horse and eventually with her high school sweetheart, who loved deeply and completely but far away. I don't see the same way as any of the others. For me, it's always mystery, always a haunted revisiting of our past, trying to understand what happened. If I really did look through four windows all together, would I discover the shining sun of who our mother really was? Or merely the hazy moon of what she is now? Would looking through each of their quarters give insight to a whole person I had missed, whom we have just now declared legally incompetent? It seemed like there ought to be other choices, that this choice, for all its good intentions, is a lose-lose for our mother and for us, though it's disguised as a win.

I take another sip of cheap beer. Maybe it was the right thing to do, but what if all the benefits of Medicaid could have been offered in her home? That option never surfaced. Why is that? The truth I'm getting to slowly: this system is hard on families. To hire lawyers, petition doctors and courts, create poverty—all to get good care. Trying to do right and all the while feeling like we are doing the wrong and shameful thing. I have called it betrayal, but what if betrayal is only one-quarter truth and other views, other windows, might be as relevant.

The four quarter windows hang out in our imaginations a while, but nothing inspiring surfaces. Our words, like our ideas, thin out to nothing. We finish our beers. We look at each other, rise, and head for the door. I suspect we all hope that this next part, where we move Mom to that once-dreaded, full-scale nursing home, will be easier than today. But we know, at least Marijo and I know, that it will be harder. It is like thinking that four quarters makes a dollar and finding out that it doesn't add up to that at all.

THE BREEZY

My mom isn't sure why she is saying so many goodbyes. *Goodbye and thank you. I've forgotten your name, but it was so good to see you.* Big smiles. She isn't sure what to make of her room being empty. She fingers her tissues until they turn to soft white wads. She isn't sure of any color or taste or scent or sound except something is happening and it's making her nervous. She keeps looking at me, questions she cannot express held in her eyes. Kathy and Lydia and Kim and Susan and Therese gather in the front room, hug her, and tell her how much they've enjoyed having her with them. Kathy tears up a little. Lydia touches my shoulder fondly. I bundle Mom into a big warm blanket, and for the last time, we push the Breezy through that warning doorbell at the door of the Manor, and we are outside, in the cool September air.

"Are we going to lunch?" She's maybe hoping for McDonald's.

"We're going right next door, Mom, to the medical care facility."

She goes quiet. I focus on the wheels, this wheelchair, this rolling cart, these fortunate circular legs that ease her across the parking lot to the much larger parking lot, to the facility. The surface is not easy; the journey, short as it is, takes muscle, but it's easier than renting an ambulance to transport her the length of a football field. We bump over the curb, and then I am shoving her Breezy up the slow incline, leaning forward, using my own legs to gain momentum over the asphalt incline, cracks and seams pocked with weeds.

"Where are we going?" Her voice again, plaintive.

I'm breathless. Pushing. *Well, Mom, I'm kidnapping you. I'm taking you away, rolling you out onto the highway a mile away, and you can take this beautiful old contraption of a wheel chair, this Breezy, and you can wheel it out onto the concrete surface and use the highway as a runway, you can speed north down old US 31, faster and faster, cross the bridge over the Hart River, your wild white hair flying in the wind, and if we do this right, that chair will get going so fast, you will lift into that wild blue, levitate with wheels spinning like tops, your Breezy will rise in the breezes, and you will escape from us all, breezing out over these buildings, around this small American town, out over the apple and peach orchards, over the asparagus and bean fields, the stone-laden cemetery and brick church, and you will follow the old familiar way down Jackson Road, you will pass the gray farmhouses of friends you grew old with, pass over the loam fields that always are freshly tilled in your mind, the wide stretches of woods and pasture that defined you, and you will fly over them, over the cedar swamp, the irrigation pond, and over the familiar white farmhouse with its grand silver maple, over our red-gabled barns with their ghost animals, over the rusted sprawling machinery, back to the bustle that you were once the volcanic center of, back to your spinning life. You and your Breezy will ride the currents of time, and escape, hair streaming, wheels spinning in the wind.*

"Next door, Mom," and I giggle maniacally, and push harder up the slow incline, past the smokers' tree, past the convalescent unit, over the darkened potholes. And then we are there, at the industrial-style entrance to the sprawling modern building. I hit the auto switch, and the double glass doors swing open into the long hallway, the lobby hall, which is loud and cold with high ceilings that make it a box canyon. I push Mom and her Breezy inside and we wheel down the echoey cavern lined with narrow brocade couches. At the end, another set of doors, and we cross, her wheels turning slowly, and I wonder if there could be a colder, more awful way to enter this new life, these two sets of doors separated by this gorge of an antiseptic lobby.

And then the second set of doors swing open, and the ceiling lowers, and there, a simpler hallway, an office door, and Deb, the smiling admit person, and Amanda, Mom's social worker, and the small dog, Ladybelle, waddling among our feet, sniffing and licking toes, and she comes right to Mom, and Mom makes a small sound, and lets her arm drop, and Ladybelle licks her hand, and Mom smiles, and everyone smiles big artificial smiles, and it begins, the day of flight and spinning wheels in this new place where she will live within its walls, within its parameters, clean and bright, until she dies.

PUZZLE

The gatekeeper of the medical care facility is Michael, a middle-aged man with a graying crewcut who sits in his extrawide wheelchair right at the corner of C hall. With his elbow braced on the arm of his chair, he waves his hand like he's sawing the air, like it's a stiff flag, his fingers straight, his eyes looking into the eyes of every person who enters, and his voice on repeat, "Weelllcooommme, haaappppyyyyy Tooossday. Weelllcooommme, haaappppyyyyy Tooossday."

"Happy Tuesday, Michael," I say, and he half lifts his sentinel eyes, a neurological storm flashing over his face, not recognition exactly, but he knows I have seen him, an exchange then. It is enough. He renews his efforts, focusing on the next visitor, on his one job, with all the tenacity the stroke has left him. In these last three weeks, I have seen the nurses feeding Michael at lunch; swallowing is a task that troubles him, and even his food, pudding soft, sometimes chokes him, but this he can do, he can greet every single person who enters C hall. "Haaappppyyyyy Tooossday."

I pass the dining room, turn another corner, and Heidi, the charge nurse standing at the meds cart, sees me and says, "Oh, she's in the day room." Another corner into the bright, overdecorated room with windows on three sides, weave into these wheelchaired elders, some slack-jawed with sleep, some staring at an enormous TV—a cooking show where people with rainbow hair assemble sushi. Lots of prerecorded laughter from the TV; mixed reaction from the residents. Miss Vee, one of the wheelchair tenants, asks, "What is that stuff?" of the TV cuisine. "Looks like a turd!" she shouts at the seared tuna on the screen, just cut fresh and served on a bed of something lacey green. Of course, Miss Ardelle, who epitomizes primness, hears this one line, shakes her head at Miss Vee, once again appalled—Miss Ardelle is so good at *appalled*. Laura, an aide massaging one woman's swollen hands, giggles at this and calls over to Miss Vee, "Pipe down, darling, you'll wake the sleepers." In and out among the dozen residents, caregivers, aides, and nurses offering a variety of soft-voiced questions and answers, repeated acts of patience, little gestures. What I know so far. For all the industrial quality of a nursing facility, at last here Mom's care matches her need. They are observing, paying attention, recording temperatures and a dozen other things. The caregivers move among the residents, encouraging one to finish lunch, one to drink a little more water, another to take her pills.

And there's Mom, a perched and lonely white bird at the end of the room, slumped forward in her wheelchair, her eyes open but looking out, not in. Though she is at last receiving care she needed, since she has been here, she has become even more silent. She doesn't like my questions.

I find I have to speak to her more than ever now, but the way it must be done is that I speak to her in my mind. This is how I talk with her now. A silent direct address. Always this, you in me, me in you, those voices. Whereas once I shouted aloud, now the voice is internal.

There you are. There you are, Mom.

As these new days pass in the facility, your new home, Mom, I put together a slow picture of how it goes, put together the life we made for you, that you made for yourself, that we made for each other with resistance and misunderstanding, with fear and, yes, I see it now, emerging, abundant love. Abundant. We made these intertwined lives from that brokenness, from inadequacy, from a relationship with parts missing. Ours with you and yours with us. Abundant and inadequate. How can they be both?

Today we head for the activity room, where beautiful old women will put together a puzzle. Five or six or seven women who can still put puzzles together, or pretend that they can, will over this long afternoon, or maybe over two or three afternoons, roll their wheelchairs to the table, settle, finger the pieces into an image, then push away. Some will give up, some lose concentration and doze at the table. Some become obsessed.

I push you into place, look down at the scattered pieces.

Every day now, as you fade, I see that your care is better. We are not here with you, but the care is—physical therapy, better food—monitored and measured, and all that allows me to think more easily at last. You have more regular baths, and the odor wafting off you is of soap and antiseptic. I am beginning to think differently, Mom, about this life of mine, this life of yours, this process of aging that more and more people of my generation must put together blindly, by feel, fingering our lies, our truths, feeling the losses in the dark, that flannel of what-ifs, that crazy quilt that is how we take care of our parents. And how we take care of ourselves. You know this, Mom.

Most of the time, I suspect we wonder how the hell we could get it so wrong.

We pull into the puzzle table. Settle. The women turn busy, concentrating. They are putting together a puzzle; they don't think about death. Or they cuddle up to its mystery and solve it. Mystery. Scattered, scattered, some pieces dark, some so bright they blind.

Gretchen, who refuses the respectful "Miss" given to all the elders here, is still so mentally sharp, she can be a leader. She lifts the box cover, passes it so each elder can study the image. She dumps the puzzle pieces onto the vinyl table. The pieces tumble, soft clicking of cardboard as they fall on a hard surface, sounding like a broken hurried tick of an old clock. The dry scent of carboard rises. Gretchen shakes her head. "Five hundred pieces," she says, mildly disgusted. Three hundred is best. More than that, and the pieces tend to be too small for trembling hands. Puzzle manufacturers should know this—elders need interesting puzzle images but with fewer pieces, large enough for fading sight, arthritic or palsied fingers.

They are putting together this puzzle, pets in a garden: three puppies, four kittens, several rabbits, a couple of birds, and about a hundred flowers. Mostly, too many eyes.

Gretchen knows exactly, announces, "Eleven sets of eyes."

Mine on yours. I am putting together the puzzle of your eyes, blue with that darker star in the middle, blue that can glow, pupils surrounded by fragmentation of the iris, one eye sharper than the other, the one that no longer sees—what does it see? I am putting together this puzzle of your eyes on mine, half-seeing. I am putting together an image of your body too, puddling to the right, arm braced on a bolster, your body soft in the wheelchair, afghan draping knees, a cascade of blue and lilac. Your feet swell inside white booties. Edema. Edema.

You hate puzzles, always have. Not just bored with them, hate them. *Like watching paint dry. You can get old before you finish one of those things.* Back at the Manor, the more they encouraged you, the more you avoided them. And now, here too, you're faced with encouragement to put them together.

"Good for the brain," the nurses say.

You used to retort; now you stare at the pieces in silent subtext.

I know you will either be silent in their presence or, on a day when speech is easy, be utterly polite and say simply, *I don't care for puzzles.* But your subtext: *Get that away from me.*

We are putting together the puzzle, finding a place at this table. Can we put together the why puzzle of us? Should we?

First, we pick out the pieces with straight sides. If we put the frame together first, we get some idea of the whole, how big it is, how hard it will be.

The frame: we have tried to love each other, but there are some pieces missing. Is it possible still?

Gretchen realizes, "I think we put this one together before."

And Elinore says, "A hundred times."

And Miss Ardelle says, "We did?"

And Miss Vee says, "Well I don't know. Did we?"

Gretchen says, "Can't be helped. Let's do it again." She is putting together her own puzzle of head tremors, but with steady enough

hands, she can sort the puzzle pieces, straight sided and interlock-
ing. Somehow, she keeps track of the pieces despite her tremors.

Miss Betty, another elder in a wheelchair, enters the activity
room, rolling forward by steadily shuffling her feet. She approaches
the windows slowly, with reverence, watering can tilted in her lap.
She is putting together the puzzle of white and purple and lavender African violets on the wide windowsill. This is the best moment of her day. Everyone stops and watches this best moment. It's
like a prayer. Or the longest moment of our lives. She lifts the can
slowly, leaning forward over her knees, stretching her hands forward, hovering over the delicate blossoms, the velvety leaves. One
by one, she waters a couple dozen potted plants dotted with those
church colors, pours water into the darkness of dirt. She knows just
how much. Then she deadheads the plants, gathering the dry blossoms in her palm. We all watch, exploring her prayer with our eyes.
Is this love, the simple tending of living things? Plants? Humans?
The puzzles, great and small. I still ask every day. When Betty's done
watering every single violet, she turns to us, nods, and rolls out. The
invocation is complete. Amen.

Now we begin the puzzle in earnest.

Memory rises again, as it does so often now with my mother, re-
shaping before my eyes. Today, I remember water. Watering. A process not only for plants. Hot days on those long-past fields, sweating and dust drenched. Mom took turns sending each of us out of
the fields and back to the house, to the well, to turn on the spigot,
to fill the jug, to bring water back to her, to the workers, to her
children who had worked alongside her, not always willingly. We
shoved the hose into the mouth of the jug and let it run until the
water burst up, flushing out the tepid, turning so cold it hurt. We
let it overflow, stood in bare feet, stood in the wet grass until we had
to turn again to the heat of the harvests. She must have known that
we took our time, would scold us when we lugged the jugs back.
"What took you so long?" But she nodded when we handed up the
jugs, dripping with condensation. And to pass that cool water, to

pass it among the workers, to pass it mouth to mouth, was connection as sweet as kissing.

We all turn to the multieyed puzzle, to the mystery of all these cardboard fragments. The eyes of animals. Pets in a garden. Eleven sets of eyes. More if you count the eyelike center of flowers. Eyes as old and watery as . . . water in a milk jug. Putting together a pattern. A pattern broken. A pattern reformed. Mystery, a different one every day, a different clue in every piece. Five hundred pieces.

Find the frame before we die.

The first piece I pick up is a prayer gone wrong. A single complete eye without a face. I don't like this piece. Even if prayer is all magical thinking, it begins with earnest intention. A sending up of attention. Do you see me? Do I see you? I set aside an eye.

I place a couple of frame pieces in front of you, Mom, and you finger them, pushing them close, turning them over, and putting them near to each other. Your brain does not let you lift them together to make the lock. But you know they seem right near each other. You know too, they ought to fit. We ought to fit, but we don't. We are pieces of different puzzles. You can't fit them together. Should I reach over, do it for you? Would you let me? Have you forgotten how this goes, this hopeless feeling of putting together something that is not a match? You who put together so much from inadequate materials. Do you even want to put together this puzzle, you who hated puzzles?

Now I am putting together the puzzle within the puzzle, with all the other puzzle women here in the activity room. We gather near the windows where the light brightens our table, our laps. We study the fragmented images. The animals' ears and paws, the plants, the eyes. Here, a piece of rose, of peony, of your damaged and earth-shaping love, which I learned to obey and fear. Here, the spray of clinging vine on a fence, puzzle of good work and hard shame and, yes, some boundary. Perhaps a frame? Here, also the weedy rebellions—all the same nettled color, our mutual cruelty. What if it's two-sided, this puzzle? This prayer? Every piece of you, the other side is me. One side always facing away. Which side is which? Time has made it all one puzzle, an image I put together every day, even when I am not with you.

At the table, you let two pieces touch each other, two pieces shape now a part of the puzzle frame dense with garden leaves, a part of the garden without the wildly blooming flowers or eyes but dense with green. I watch: *Mom, just lock them together, one piece to another.* But you push them apart as though they were magnets, repelling. This too is prayer.

You lift your eyes and study the puzzle of women gathered at the table surface, silently working the pieces. You watch what they do, then push your pieces at each other as they do. The pieces touch, a jig to jig, like a friend might just touch a friend's shoulder. Maybe it begins with that old wish, me wanting to be friends. I always wanted you to be my friend, but you saw every weakness in me, and then of course, I lied to you, more than once, more than twice, and because of that, you never trusted me. The eyes of that cat tell a sad truth.

I am putting together the puzzle of our not being friends now that you are nearly a child. How does this work? Too late, and with so many mistakes, all this love scattered at our fingertips, the pieces to the puzzle we cannot put together, and yet, if we study it, could we see how, you and I? Could we put together the vision, here at the puzzle table? One eye at a time. Could we see how we see each other, the eyes looking back at us? One I, one eye at a time. Would the two find a single face?

Here at the puzzle table, the women murmur and go quiet, murmur and go quiet. Stack the eyes, make guesses as to which eyes go with which.

Now you push the two pieces of green toward each other. You place them on top of each other. Turn both upside down. I tell myself not to help, not to do anything to interfere with your concentration. Your wrists are braced on the table, and you look up, at the other women, watching them again. You sigh a long sleeve of breath.

"Mom, do you want to go?"

You look at me, eyes watery. "No," you say. You look away.

"You like the puzzle?" I'm looking for confirmation.

"No," you say, almost exasperated—that old disapproval. *How could I be so stupid?* Then you know you must explain something; you're not sure what, how. Finally, "I like it here." You nod toward the women. I look at them, all bent to the work, piecing together. The light shines on the faded heads, gathered over the daily work of the puzzle. Ah, we are a gathering. We are putting together the puzzle of gathering. Of being together. These *togetherings*. That is not mystery. Is it comfort? I look at her face; it is not unhappy. Let it pass for comfort then. We are together putting the whole picture together as best we can. You reach for the puzzle pieces, and after a long and perilous struggle, your fingers brailling over the edges, you lock them together. They are not made for each other, but they do hold.

MY MOTHER'S COUNTRY

In the country of age, I toss slippers, shove aside my mother's recliner, ransack her tiny room, searching for her afghan, the blanket of my betrayal. Uppercase *Afghan* is the term preferred by the people of Afghanistan, a country you can find on a map. The eponymous lowercase *afghan* is the blanket gone missing from my mother's room, part of this country that will not show up on any map except the map of being and not being. Still, I have learned: this place claims its own culture, rules, laws, language. For years now, I have skirted its boundaries, entering as often as I can, knowing it is my country too, but not my home. Not yet. For her it is both, country and now home, and never home. But here, here is where it ends.

"I'm so cold." Her voice, an anxious child.

Not under the bed, not under the pillow. I stop, step out into the hall to look for an aide; it is that imperative. How do we live without the afghan? No matter how young or old you are, those soft-yarned, zigzagged, old-world, hand-knitted or crocheted blankets draped over your grandma's chair offer not just warmth but an age-old security, connection, family. And no matter that the blanket style originated in a country the crocheters might not easily find on a map, those crocheters will tell you, counting stitches as they go, those zigzags warm the cold nights.

Still, it's a generationally dated term, perhaps no longer politically correct. Because when I enlist the aide to help me, a young woman with a degree so fresh that she can use her ID card for a mirror, she doesn't know what I'm talking about as I rifle my mother's closet. I mutter into Mom's seasonal sweatshirts—snowflake, maple leaf, daisy print—"The afghan was here yesterday."

I turn, read her face. Translate. "Where's her throw?"

A dawning. "Oh, that. Gotta be there somewhere." *Throw* the young aide understands, but she strides out anyway. I stand at the closet, empty-handed. My mother will not know what I mean if I call her afghan a *throw.*

I'll cover you with a throw.

Do you want your throw?

Throw me the throw.

What are we throwing here? Her afghan is what she wants.

A nurse pops in, "Got a problem?"

I nod, ask, "Do you know where Mom's throw went?"

"Throw? You mean her afghan? Check between the wall and the bed. They get lodged."

I catch a glimpse of purple, soft wool crumpled at the foot of the bed, tangled under gray sheets and comforter, yank it free. Her afghan is pretty, all Mom's favorite hues in those zigzags: soft purple, lavender, pale blue, pink, and then a broad row of cream, and then the purple, lavender, pale blue, pink again in back and forth diagonals. I shake it out, tuck it over her lap and around her legs, making sure the afghan does not drag under her chair's wheels. I kneel in front of her and begin our liturgy. "Who made this for you, Mom?"

"Oh, Mama made it." She perks up. She means Grandma Julia, dead of pneumonia in 1983 at ninety-three. My grandmother made afghans for every child, grandchild, niece, nephew, church group, and fundraiser in the county. And for not a few pets.

"And when did she have time to do that?"

"Last week. She can just crochet. After ... peaches." It's August she knows, peach season.

"And how many quarts of peaches did you two put up?"

She looks at me. She knows I want a number. She starts, pauses, turns her hands in her lap, and I realize I shouldn't have used the numbers.

"You usually get about forty-eight quarts, don't you?"

"That many?"

"I'm not sure, but that seems right. Does it seem right to you?"

"Out of a bushel?"

"No, two." The requisite number of bushels we canned each summer.

"But I thought...oh shoot." She senses something, looks around. "Is this my room?"

Quick now, before she gets anxious. "Shall we blow this pop stand?"

She studies me closely and repeats softly, "Blow the pop stand?" She has lost most idiomatic metaphor, but still, like an old scent, she recognizes humor's tone, and she knows it's her turn to respond. "Blow this pop stand," she repeats with commitment.

I sign Mom out. Since she can no longer make the transfer from wheelchair to car, our options are limited for this lunch I have promised her off campus. Down the hall, me swerving the chair a bit to make her laugh, the big automated lobby doors swing open, and we're in the parking lot, struck with August heat. Mom sighs in relief, "Oh that feels good," she says—this with the afghan on her lap. I retrieve two hats from my car, my big beach hat for her. She looks like a great white gardenia on wheels.

I bumble her wheelchair along Hart's crumbling sidewalks for five blocks to the Lakeside Café. We can usually find a place on the back patio where she can watch Hart Lake's dark slow water, facing away from the other tables so no one will see what a mess she makes now as she hangs on to her last physical ability, feeding herself, left-handed (she's right-handed), with a spoon. Once I tried it myself. By the time I had to brush my lunch off my lap, I felt only admiration.

But after jolting her down walks that have buckled and cracked, we find the café unexpectedly closed. She goes into martyr speak: "Oh it's all right, I'm fine." If I wheel her back, lunch at the facility will be over and she will be hungry, and they will be bothered in the kitchen and give her a PB&J and milk. I wipe the sweat off my face. I adjust her hat, adjust mine.

The only option? Down the block, Kristi's Pour House, a local dive that smells of spilled beer and fried food and could qualify for the Antarctic research station, the air-conditioning is so high. I remember a side room where we might sit and no one would trip over this lug of a wheelchair. I see Mom's face taking on the distant look—she's slipping back into her broken mind, and I can't bear to let her go just yet. Quick now. I ease the wheelchair down the curb, rattle our way over cracked concrete, dodge a couple of cars, up the other curb, and through the boot-scuffed aluminum storm door into the dark space. The patrons, coveralled out-of-work men and a couple of ciggy-scented women, seeing us struggle over the threshold, slide their heavy bodies off the stools and become more than kind, shoving tables and chairs as we negotiate our way to the side room. Even the regulars, leaning out from the booths, scoot out of the way. *Can ya make it? Sure ya okay?* Once settled in the side room, the sweet waitress opens the side door to the street and the hot air rushes in, warming the space. At my look, she shrugs, *Aw, what the hell*, in reference to the air-conditioning. Mom can see the traffic, the comings and goings of the town, and this will occupy her. We are fine.

I order soup for her, chicken noodle, and when it comes, thick old-fashioned egg noodles crowd the broth. I break up the noodles so they won't slide off her spoon. I feed her often but when we are out like this, she wants to feed herself as much as she can.

"Ummm, good," and she tucks right in. After a while, she lifts her head, straight white hair glowing in the gray light. She studies the room, then asks, "Is this a bar?"

I brace myself. It's not that she minds bars, but for all the memory she has lost, certain proprieties remain indelible as tattoos. We are here in the middle of a weekday, not Friday night fish fry for Catholics, which was the appropriate time she and Dad patronized our local bar. I don't know if she will object, this woman who once walked out of a restaurant for being owned by people whose political views were so far left she thought they might be communists. That, and they served pork chops with garlic instead of apples.

"Yes, Mom, it's a bar."

"I thought so." She nods like she's figured out something. She inhales a long noodle, broth spilling from the spoon.

I brace myself and ask, "How do you feel about that?"

"Oh, real good." She nods, slurps her soup.

I smile. "Well then, would you like a beer?"

"Oh no. I couldn't." She puts her spoon down like that's final.

I decide right then I'll have a beer. "You want some of mine?"

"Are you gonna?"

I know what that means. "I'm gonna have something Belgian." This appeals to her national pride, her Belgian ancestry.

"Well, a little sip." She raises her eyebrows: how daring.

I order a pint of Blue Moon and a highball glass on the side. When it comes, I pour off a third, tuck in a straw, and hold it up to her lips. She wraps her lips around it and sucks. And sucks, and it's gone. I pour in the rest, and over the course of the lunch, she drinks it all. My mother has not had a drink in years, not by choice, but because alcohol exacerbates her incontinence. But now that she wears heavy-duty pull-ups every day, it's a moot point, isn't it? I don't care: I'm thrilled she's enjoying a beer. It's the smallest of adventures, the simplest of forays into normalcy, a momentary reprieve. I know the aides will have to deal with the results, and I should be ashamed of myself, but to see her draw on that beer with such intensity makes my eyes smart.

Before we know it, lunch is over.

To go out means to come back.

To return to that other country.

During the trek back, she dozes, no doubt because of the beer. Even after pushing her wheelchair up the slow rise away from the lake, I'm not quite ready to let her succumb to the two-hour nap that will be in order if the aides have their way. And though she cries a little when we reenter the building, she's seems alert. We roll out to the facility's enclosed patio, where the trees offer sweet shade, a little breeze. Bucket-grown cherry tomato plants are ripening in a row. I steal a couple tomatoes, hand them to her. She chews, and I am so glad that the tastes of certain foods have not faded for her.

"These are . . ." and she holds the question up in the tiny tomato.

"Cherry tomatoes," I say.

"Cherries? Taste like tomatoes."

"They are, but little, like cherries. So, they're called cherry tomatoes."

She lets out a little giggle. "The joke's on us," she says.

These small survivals of the wrecked mind awe me. How did she know it was a small joke? Because it's related to taste? I wish I understood how it worked, what would stay and what would go, and what would stay if exercised. I used to ask everyone: charge nurses and aides, the doctor who sees her twice a month, the occupational or physical therapist, guy who does foot care, woman who plays organ for hymn sings, volunteer who brings her Holy Communion. No one can tell me from one week to the next what she will know. Sometimes she seems to be searching her own mind, her face reflective and intense, as though she recognizes an absence but the tool to name it is also gone, lost in the gray flannel zigzags of the mind. She has become progressively more silent, more unable to shape sentences, though on some days conversation suddenly succeeds, and she can say a whole thing. I realize she's having a very good day; today she is as with me as she can be. I am suddenly laughing.

"Yeah, some joke, right Mom."

We sit in the sun; her head drops forward. Here is another locale in the country of age: the shared silence, the drift of time between us. It is both thin and lush here, full of thought spinning its bright frayed edges, *why* and *because* at the very same moment they both disintegrate. We are together, often holding hands, and when she looks up, bleary-eyed, she sees me like seeing me for the first time. Her eyes open wide in surprise and her mouth forms a silent *Oh*. And I see her. Oh. Because of all the terrible times we had, tearing each other apart, I cherish this sudden recognition. We still recognize each other, her criteria for living. As long as you know me.

I roll her chair toward the protected aviary to bird-watch, to sidle up to where the finches are whispering to each other, where she can nap, where I can sit next to her in this implacable silence. It seems no matter how positively I think, this country is all about loss. We do not survive it, so each time, I relearn a way to live inside it.

An aide pushes out and parks a rolling recliner, basically a La-Z-Boy set high on wheels that operates like a wheelchair but with the comfort of a recliner. A gray-haired, fierce-looking woman with darkly freckled skin reclines on this chair. She is restless, talk-singing to herself, opening her hands and closing them in a gesture that seems familiar, like a conductor's. I make eye contact and say hello, and she commences a proclamation, a string of nonsense in a commanding voice. She laughs, not manic but warm. Then sudden anger. She stares me down. I am someone she knows; I am a stranger.

What is she seeing?

Was she once a performer, now looking for her lost audience?

I take out my notebook and wave my pen in the air as if writing, asking her permission. She smiles in delight and nods, then shakes her head as if in argument, then nods again. Assent. As the warm afternoon wanes, while my mother doses, her afghan on her knees, I transcribe what this woman sings from her high recliner.

I want to be alive today, I do.

I want to be alive today so I can be alive tomorrow.

Tomorrow I have a . . .

Tomorrow I want to marry . . . tomorrow.

Here, she looks at me, and suddenly scolds me.

What are you talking about . . .

I don't know who . . .

With great seriousness she sings:

Might be four, might be five, might be six, might be seven.

Might be eight. Might be ten.

I know more . . . no I don't want to tell . . . tidy tidy tidy

Tomorrow, tomorrow.

Her *tomorrows* go two ways: like the tomorrows in Shakespeare's *Macbeth*, the sonorous *tomorrow and tomorrow and tomorrow* speech, where the future *creeps in its petty pace . . . to the last syllable of recorded time . . .* where Macbeth realizes the consequences of his actions. But then, an entirely different voice, the bright tomorrow song from the musical Annie. *Tomorrow, tomorrow. I love you, tomorrow.* Then numbers. *Might be eight, might be ten.* A jump rope game? The words bridge into metaphor, into days or years of tomorrows. To counting and losing count. They imply all our yesterdays. My pen stills, and I listen, my mother sleeping beside me, the woman's chorus of tomorrows on continuous repeat. Her song is the long-patterned afghan of this place. Safe body, weakened mind. Beauty and efficiency, compliments and silence, heaven and death. Counting and coming to the end of counting. Tomorrow and tomorrow. Mine and hers. Zigzag.

My mother rouses. I ask if she wants water, and she nods, and looks up, "I heard singing."

"Yes, the lady was singing." I nod to the woman, now fading into almost inaudible murmurings.

"I wasn't sure. I thought . . ." She drifts off.

She thought what? Was she someplace else, in the heaven she fears? She looks down, studies the afghan. Her face seems resigned and . . . what? Not to overstate, a little like the face of Mary in Michelangelo's *Pietà*, that eternal sadness in the tilt of her head, though Mary's face is marble smooth and my mother's crosshatches nine decades.

She looks down, accepting, searching, accepting, searching. Her fingers cling to the yarn.

"Who made that for you, Mom," I ask, touching the darkest purple, the color of betrayal.

She looks up. "Grandma did." She still knows. Except she doesn't. She does not remember when her mother, my Grandma Julia, fell in our mudroom of the farmhouse, and Mom could no longer lift her. She does not remember that Grandma came here, to this facility, for her last three years before she died of a sudden pneumonia. My mother does not remember searching her own heart.

Do we all betray the ones we love?

Do we do the best we can inside this country of our own making?

Now, we both have our hands on the afghan, tracing the back and forth, the soft sky colors. Fingers on the diagonals.

Here's another betrayal. Her original afghan was so riddled with moth holes and stained with spilled coffee and scented with urine that my sister and I burned it when we moved her here. The afghan she fingers now I found at Vintage Rose, the Christian resale shop in town. The day I found it, I wasn't sure I could pull off the deception. Not even the same colors. But the afghan pattern is the same and that's what she saw, what she embraced, what we could rely on to get her, us, through the move. That zigzag, those back-and-forth diagonals, first one way, then the other, an ancient design borrowed from the other side of the world. She tracks the zigzag with her long fingers, follows these tomorrows, the dark and the bright, death and heaven, drinking a beer and peeing her pants. She studies it closely, as if for the first time. Tomorrow or tomorrow. Hers and mine. Tender and terrible. And common. She recognizes the pattern and claims it as her own. Oh Mama. I reach in, take her hand, our fingers tangled in the interconnected colors, claim it with her.

EPILOGUE:
PANDEMIC 2020

Ten years since my father's last breath. Mom turns ninety-nine today, April 28, 2020. Early spring or late winter in Michigan, cold and dreary. Mom still lives in the Oceana County Medical Care Facility. She does not walk at all, does not talk much—only a few scattered scripted words. She now has a suprapubic catheter, is fed by the staff, is blind in one eye, and is unable to answer any but the most basic questions. We do not know how she continues. We do not know how to live with this fact that she continues. Her smile could light the world.

I stand in the foyer in front of the glass doors, watch the long hall at the medical care facility. At the far end of the hall, an aide rounds the corner, and there she is, small body rolling ever closer in her Breezy, a patterned comforter over her knees, her white blouse stretching across her tummy, the embroidery distorted, elongating the flowers. The aide rolls her close to the door and I touch the glass. She does not move but looks at me quietly.

"Hi Mom. Happy Birthday."

By now, her criteria for living, *as long as I know you*, once hailed for its clarity, has revealed its vagaries, its blue-toned uncertainties. Because it turns out there is a gray zone, a half knowing on her part coupled with an unknowing on our parts. What if sometimes she does, and sometimes she doesn't, and what if she knows different people at different times? And what if we do not really recognize her for who she has become now—do not know her as she would want us to. *Knowing* is an uncertainty roiling inside our visits. I live with this new understanding. Sometimes we are connected to people we love and still can't really know anything.

Some days she knows me completely, some days she knows me if I say my name. Then that flicker, her one good eye takes me in, appraising like the judge again, then that half-smile of acknowledgment—and we are back at the farmhouse table, sorting buttons, and the world is round and whole.

Until the pandemic.

More often now, she is only certain that I am someone who likes her or who maybe loves her, probably one of her children, but, well, one can't be sure and maybe she should just take a nap and not think about it. I am from that other life that on some days she can almost touch, almost remember that there was someone else who she was . . . and from that life, someone has come to see her.

She responds differently to my siblings. Tom and Rick say she doesn't know who they are at all and hasn't for a long time. Pat is far away in Colorado, but Pat says that when she and Duane come to Mom in summers, Mom sometimes calls Pat by name. During last summer's visit Pat and Duane played fifties dance music and danced for Mom, and she watched them and laughed and was present. She knew them sort of, but she really knew their daughter, Emily, in the height of her youth. Mom recognized that beauty, and in that, knew Emily.

For years now, Marijo and I have made weekly visits to Mom, Marijo often more than once a week. Mom knows us, if cloudily. Sometimes, she seems to remember Brooke, Marijo's daughter. But recently, it is only me she knows. Sort of. This hurts Marijo, and we have tried to figure out why it is me she seems to know—or if I am even reading the signs correctly. Because I am the oldest? Or because I hurt her more than the others? Or because I repeatedly tell her stories about her own fields, her own children, about the farm and the gardens. I say over and over, often the same stories, "Remember Mom, when . . ." She once looked straight at me and said,

"You're the one who remembers things..." but she didn't sound happy about it.

Now, Mom's birthday, April 28, in a year like no other, a year that distorts the numerical significance of ninety-nine. What is one shy of a hundred years when half a million people are gone untimely early? I last saw Mom in early February, before the pandemic. I visited the facility with her usual lunch, McDonald's fries and one of those dried out cheeseburgers that, when I warmed it up in the microwave, released its artificially smoky scent. I cut up the burger into eighths, squeezed the pieces closed so it became gooey finger food. She could pick up a piece and lift it, trembling, to her mouth and murmur like a gentle animal.

Then I left her for a month. David and I traveled to Guatemala, a long-planned trip to work at the Safe Passage program in Guatemala City on the edge of the dump, and to tour the volcano country. For a month. My greatest dread was that Mom would take a turn and it would be hard to get a plane back to Hart, that she would die without me there. I talked with Mom's nurses. *She's fine*, they assured me. She had been so slow in decline that her slope had nearly leveled, and the incremental losses were almost immeasurable, and that state passed for stability. *Go*, they said, *have a good time*.

I didn't count on flu, what we called it at first. I even enjoyed the pun of the early description: a novel virus, a coronavirus. Crown. Then, ever more serious news. Contagious. Possibly deadly. Spreading quickly.

I start calling the medical care facility every day.

They are aware. They are watching. She's still fine. They're all fine.

One morning, as I watch a green heron fledge among Lake Atitlán's shoreline cattails, the radio blares that the World Health Organization has declared the virus at pandemic stage. I linger over the word, strangely new and biblical at the same time—*pandemic*. Pandemics are epidemics on steroids, aren't they? Pandemics are a kind of plague, aren't they? We don't have plagues in this world, not since the Black Death in medieval times.

The young heron drops into the shallows, stands on spindle legs, learning its footing in the mud along the shore. It's awkward, trying out the murky waters, making its way among stalks.

My thoughts shift slowly, pulling up history. We do have plagues, but not for a hundred years or so. What they called the Spanish flu, but it was not from Spain, though it too probably jumped from animals. Some thirty million people worldwide died in two plus years. Nothing since. No, that's not true either. My own history rises slowly: the polio epidemic. Though it was in the United States from the early 1900s, polio surged in the 1940s and 1950s, killing or paralyzing over a half million, until the Salk vaccine came into being. I even remember the long lines at our county courthouse, children lined up for the sugar cube that held immunity. Then the AIDS crisis in the 1980s. I was at the height of my sexual prowess—and learned to carry and use condoms, whether the guy wanted to or not. AIDS killed or infected around a quarter million people in ten years—and still infects people today. There was SARS in 2003. Of the eight thousand or so people who were sickened, nearly 10 percent died. Ebola surged to epidemic status in Africa in 2014. Of the thirty thousand cases identified, again about 10 percent died. Only eleven cases in the United States. This outbreak led to President Obama's commission on Global Health Security and Biodefense, which worked until 2017, when it was partially disbanded and many members were not replaced. All of these epidemics had been stopped with measures that at the time were considered draconian. But they had been contained. The difference here? COVID-19 appeared to be uncontained, therefore pandemic.

As I watch the fledged heron, the word takes on form and confidence. How do we learn to walk, breathe in this new time of pandemic? I start to pack, one ear always to the radio.

The next day, President Trump declares a national state of emergency—though by then we know. This is plague and we, all of us, are caught in its vortex. David and I need to go home. Now. Somewhere in the flurry of packing, I realize that once home, I will have to quarantine. I will not be able to see Mom for yet another two weeks. Totaling six weeks.

Will she remember me?

I'm hoping for a last glimpse of the green heron when Marijo's number shows up on the cell: *Hello, hello, what's wrong?*

Mom's fine, she says first. She knows my worst fear because it is also hers. We won't be with her when she passes. The gist this time: Mom's facility is going into lockdown, a quarantine that will go on for the duration of the pandemic—we cannot see our mother at all.

And now it is her birthday. April 28. Three months since I last saw her. Marijo and I talk over morning coffee. We both tear up over the fact that we can't see her on her ninety-ninth birthday, that it has been so long it seems like a dark forever. I ask her: if I drove down, could we go to her bedroom window and talk through glass? Marijo says maybe, but I can tell by her voice that it's almost harder for her to see Mom behind glass, unable to touch her, than not to see her at all. I understand. But after I hang up, I sit on the couch and sip cold coffee and let the silence talk. David looks up from his computer news and says, "Yeah, you should go anyway." He knows my heart.

Which is how I end up driving the two hours to the facility on nearly empty highways, stopping only once at a roadside garden nursery, where I point to a tiny blue globe with moss tucked in at its north pole, and with gloved hands, they lift and wrap and carry it out to the curb, and I mask up, and leaving the car running, pick it up. All the long drive, I think of her, of days like moss in a blue globe, days as quiet as wonder can be when you listen to it before the spring leaves come.

When I pull into the parking lot, I wrap the vase in two disinfectant wipes, and put on my mask, and call the nurses from the car. An aide will bring her to the door. I am buzzed into the closed foyer, the glass laden with signs warning of the automatic door, now locked, of the quarantine, the lockdown, that residents can be reached via their social worker. Protocol and procedure.

Now Mom is at the glass. She stares through these tempered windows, looks at me as though she should know me. The aide smiles, adjusts the chair so Mom can see me better through glass. She looks unsteadily in my direction. Just below her body, the words "Automatic Door" form a decorative barrier between us. The glass is fingerprinted—others have done this—but still reflections play in and out.

"Hi Mom. Happy birthday," I say.

She can't hear through the glass. She looks at the aide, and the aide repeats, "She says happy birthday, Ruth."

My mother looks back at me, says, "Oh. Thank you." Proper.

She studies my face, studies the glass, studies my face again. She is trying to figure out who I am.

"It's Anne," I say. "It's me." A ridiculous thing to say.

She says nothing. She studies the glass. Am I blurred or distorted like one of those carnival mirrors? I explain that we've been gone, that we have been quarantined, that the state is in lockdown. The aide repeats everything I say because Mom can't hear through the muffling of the glass.

I say, "I'm sorry we couldn't come to see you sooner. It's because of this sickness."

When the aide repeats it all, Mom turns her face toward me, but doesn't speak. She has that pursed look: she knows she's supposed to say something but she's decided to keep her mouth shut on purpose.

I tell Mom about the plant, the blue globe and the delicate moss. I show her. I tell the aide I'll leave it wrapped in the wipes on the table for that purpose, and when I go out of the enclosed foyer, she can come pick it up, use the extra wipes I have not touched, and give it to Mom. She promises.

I tell Mom about our new garden, and I remember her own garden to her, the raccoons that took all of our sweet corn just as it ripened, the year I was ten, a tale I have remembered to her a dozen times. She looks at the aide as though she does not understand. I tell her about David—thinking she may remember him, connect.

The aide repeats the words, but Mom doesn't respond. Her lids go heavy.

I ask, "Mom, how old are you?"

When the aide asks, Mom opens her eyes. She thinks. She says, "About eighty."

I tell her she is ninety-nine.

She says, "Oh no." She looks at me accusingly, then down at the comforter and sighs. I have gone down the wrong road. Again. She is tired; she won't remember.

Does she know me?

Suddenly I know she doesn't. The lockdown, the long absence has done it. For a time, my identity was a loose thread she could still catch, pull through the crowded fabric of memory, but now it has disappeared, twisted into a maelstrom of knotted thought. In the larger scheme of national death and illness and loss, for the grief of so many lost lives, what happens between my mother and me is the smallest thing. But in the scheme of that small world, I had hoped that she would remember, if not me, someone. Marijo or Pat, Tom or Rick, and that long-ago phrase *as long as I know you* would hold her and hold us to her until we could be present to her again. Now I know. If the virus or anything from plain flu to kidney failure strikes, we let her go.

The aide is quiet.

I tell the aide I will say goodbye now. I tell Mom that I'll try to come again. I tell her that I love her. "I love you, Mama." The aide says to her, "She loves you." An echo without inflection. Mom does not respond, even when the aide repeats it. I thank the aide, place the plant on the table, and turn to go. Then I turn back and try to get her face in my mind, the pale skin, the crown of white hair, the weary blue eyes. I wave. Wave again. Nothing. Then. Just as I turn, her voice rises, calls me like a bell to a meal, as clearly as if she were merely eighty, "Thanks for coming, honey."

I stand still, stunned. The aide smiles—this came without prompting.

Honey is not my name, but no one else in the world calls me that.

No one could—I wouldn't let them. No one else could speak that line and turn it into the golden thread. Because whoever I am to her, in this she sees me as an intimate and uses an endearment reserved only for those in the family. My name gone, yes, but the sweetness of the tribe, her inner circle, remains. She does not know me; she is the only one who knows me. Because of her, I have come, am coming to know myself as slowly as she is leaving.

And suddenly, the memories wash over me like a lake, and at last the sense of her immense love, her generosity, her complicated caregiving, controlling ways, her breath of mind with mine—oceanic. That she can break the grip of dementia for this one cast-out line.

And then the now. These are the things I know now. We are separate humans, and we are old but undeclared friends who no longer touch. Or we are old friends touching through the glass of memory. We are mother and daughter, bonded—an untouchable, broken, repaired, unwieldy, touching bond that came from land and time and work and defiance. We are set in stone; and yet we had changed a bit with every visit, coming to know that she and I were made of different materials that only now have worn smooth enough to be near each other without combusting. It is the act of caring that has made this possible, the long drive, the scripted speech, the silence, especially the silence.

Thanks for coming, honey. A statement of gratitude. I leave the small globe of the plant but carry this away, her gift to me on her ninety-ninth birthday.

That was April. I saw my mother in person again in August when the numbers were at their lowest, a half an hour visit out of doors and at a distance of ten feet. Her wheelchair was tucked into a small table, I sat at another. Both of us were masked. I was a shadow of shadow of memory, some cloud at a distance. She didn't understand.

Then Marijo and I saw her together in September through a window in the day room. She never woke. We saw her again in early October, another outdoor masked visit during which she was awake, somewhat alert, and during which she asked three times, "Aren't you girls cold?" meaning she was cold. She never called either of us by name. She lasted maybe ten minutes. Four times through eight months of pandemic. Each time, knowing seemed less and less likely.

In early autumn, with the resurgence of cases in eldercare facilities, the activities department of the facility organized FaceTime visits on our phones. Once a week the aides called, set up a tablet on Mom's tray. We could see each other's faces. Mom didn't always know what was going on and these conversations lasted mere minutes. She rarely said anything, but I told her things about my life and hoped she heard a friendly voice. Once I read her my poems. She said nothing, but she did, for a while, appear to be listening.

After I ended each call, I often teared up, often felt there was no season as cold as this one, often felt grief like the pull of a weight always downward. Her silence was deepening beyond our understanding, beyond the process of knowing at all. Both Marijo and I could see it. We understood something was nearing, and at her age, death would enter her room sooner rather than later. When it did, we wanted only to be able to hold her, attend to her process. We begged the universe, *Let us be with her*. After a while, even that quiet prayer shifted. Now I prayed only that someone who loved her would be with her. Anyone in this time of quarantine. Any of her beloveds. Barring that, this was hard to say, any nurse, aide, angel.

Each week, she appears on FaceTime, paler and more silent and staring. Each time, my quiet plea: *Wait, Mom, wait until this is over, and we will do this together.*

Then, during a routine FaceTime visit in early November, she suddenly returns, fully present: uncannily chatty, speaking full sentences after months of silence.

"You're coming home for Christmas." She makes it a statement just as she once did, bossy, demanding, the voice that triggered my defiance. She just wouldn't give me a choice, insistence running to the imperative. A trigger. But it doesn't work.

What I'm slack-jawed about: a full sentence. Then several.

I find my voice, and without thinking, tell the truth. "No, Mom, this sickness is contagious. We can't come." I hate myself for this, for the truth of it.

But bless her, she's having none of it. "Oh, but you have to come home." That old doggedness. I almost can't answer, I love hearing it so much. When was the last time she demanded anything of me? When was the last time I heard this voice trying to control me, her world, anything? I embrace it, savor it like candy. "Yes, of course, yes, we'll come." I say yes to my mother, some rare joy ratcheting into my breathing.

And miraculously, she continues. "Christmas Day? What time?"

"How about five?" I'm making this up. Anything to keep her talking, keep that voice ringing in my ears.

"Come early. Four o'clock would be better to get things done."

So like her. Insist on more time, on working together. *Yes, we'll do that.* Once assured I will come at four, my mother, who has not planned anything for years, wants to plan the menu. There, Face-Timing on the counter in my kitchen, with her a hundred miles away in her wheelchair, we plan Christmas dinner, me extending every suggestion to keep her talking, to hear again that voice. And where once I would have argued, once I would have challenged or changed her plans, insisting on my superiority, I found myself delighting in her every suggestion, in giving over to it. Yes, I would bring the ham, one of those precooked spiral things. Yes, I'd ask Tom and Jill to bring the shrimp—they like to do that. Rick and Jackie will bring a big salad, maybe two—one with fruit. She says, "Marijo should make the potato rolls for the ham—because she's the only one of you who can make them rise." Pat and Duane. "Oh, they come from too far away" to contribute, she says, but I insist—"Mom, otherwise they will feel left out. Maybe appetizers?" She responds, "Oh, tell them to bring the beer. They're good at that."

Clear as a bell. Bring beer. I'm laughing, trying to keep the thrill of hearing her voice, hearing her belief that we will make this happen, yet again, after decades without it, this planning Christmas Dinner. I'm laughing and wiping tears and finally, with all the courses assigned, I ask her what she is making, and she announces without hesitation, with no sense of irony: "Angel food cake."

I didn't want it to be a too-cute premonition, didn't want its cli-chéd prescience, one of those moments of truth you can't make up though it sounds ridiculous. I didn't want the conversation, com-plete with angel food, to be the last gift. It was.

Through the second week of November, the number of facility staff and residents who tested positive for COVID-19 rose dramatically. The nurses called more often, reported that Mom was experienc-ing congestion and periodically refusing food. Her urine was dark. I asked if this was active dying. The nurse said, "No." Another call, I asked if we could get hospice back in, just for some palliative care, but the social workers said not even the hospice workers may enter. Sometime late the second week, they asked if she may be retested. We said of course, but for some reason, it wasn't scheduled until Tuesday, the seventeenth.

On Monday, November 16, during the worst surge of the COVID-19 pandemic, at a time when Oceana County had the highest num-ber of positivity cases in the state of Michigan, when the facility was on full lockdown and two dozen staff and a half dozen residents had tested positive, my mother entered a state of troubled breath-ing, and at about two thirty that afternoon, she stopped. The nurse called some fifteen minutes later. When I asked if anyone was with her—they were not sure. Meaning no. It is the final breaking.

That evening, a nurse broke the lockdown rules to let Marijo and me into the facility, masked and gloved, to see her body briefly. I held her hands and told her how much I loved her, told her I was sorry, told her over and over until her skin under my fingers warmed briefly. She was cremated a week later. Her ashes were bur-ied next to my father's in Mount Calvary Cemetery at St. Joseph's Catholic Church in Weare.

When I think about my mother's last moments, what I long to give her is my body holding her. That and a dream of the fields on the best day, a day full of sun and sweet heat, and a fierce untarnished pride and confidence. The work is done, but she is not tired; she is warm and easy in her body, in her own mind at last. Perhaps we five are there, having helped with a cherry or cucumber harvest, the bending and breaking and gathering of the green. Or perhaps we are children wrestling on the grass, playing as she watches. And as she watches, she does not worry for once, is at ease in the sunny pleasure of knowing who she is, is content at last. The world is her family, the farm, our father, and it is enough. She sees us laughing in the predusk. She sees each of us deeply and without her own past to trouble her. The time is gentled into a sacred quiet. There is gold in that late afternoon light. And we see her in that light of gratitude.

Other times, I will not lie, I most fear she had consciousness and knew that nothing in her own body was right, knew that she was not home, was in a strange bed, and that she felt the pain of shutting down, knew that she was alone and no one would ever come, not one of us, not Dad, not any lost angel. That she moaned for us. I live with these two possibilities every day. Her death certificate reads heart failure due to complications of chronic Alzheimer's. But her heart was always strong—a consistent description from physicians—and I read that bland statement, heart failure, to mean both her physical heart and her tenacious spirit. She was ninety-nine—so the years alone may have taken her. But in the end, it does not matter if she died of old age or of COVID-19, because in some ways, she died of COVID-19 anyway. That is not a claim I make easily, but here's a truth we all, our entire nation, now live with: the enforced isolation, loneliness; overworked staff, nurses, and all those aides; the closure of hospice, and all that went with it; but most of all the fact that we could not be with her, all contributed to her failing and to her dying alone. She may not have been a recorded victim, but she was a victim of the cultural pandemic. That aloneness in death. We all were. And are. And yes, in this time of pandemic, millions of us throughout the country will hold some version of this terrible contradiction in our hearts until we too die.

I will never know the truth of how she died. I had come at last to love her openly, and maybe I knew her, knew her to the degree one can know anyone. She knew me in ways I had to learn to see. The way I came to know her, through that slow process of care and memory, of "seeing," was also how I came to know myself—in all the contradictions. We are all broken and connected. She was the other half sphere of all my shaping, the blue world that completed mine, unwillingly and with fierce and generous control. Gradually she became the satellite that first saw the curve of the earth from outer space and knew it meant there was a whole. Or perhaps that's me; I can't always tell the difference.

Finis